JAMES ANDERSON

ENGLAND CRICKETER

MR VIVEK KUMAR PANDEY

Made with ♥ on the Notion Press Platform
www.notionpress.com

Contents

Foreword

Short Biography Of James Anderson & Life Style, Career etc. During Writing This Book No Character, No Religion & No Caste Are Harmed. It's Only For Study Purpose. We don't want to hurt anyone.

Preface

Author biography in English :

MY NAME IS VIVEK KUMAR PANDEY . I WAS BORN IN 30 SEP 2002,I AM FROM SURAT GUJARAT INDIA.MY DREAM WAS TO BE GOOD WRITERS ,MY FAMILY SUPPORTED ME TO SUCCESSFUL AND I CAN DO IT MY SELF.How do I write? That is a question, I believe, that can be honestly answered by me."CELEBRATING YOUNGEST WRITER AWARD WINNER IN GUJARAT 1ST RANK" MR PANDEY JI . I may think I did a good job writing something. The reader is the one who decides the quality of my writing. I do find writing to be natural to me and therefore find it to be a real challenge. My trick as a challenged writer is to do the best I can and know that I am happy with the final outcome. It may take a while to do my best and there may be quite a few problems I run into along the way.

I am not a greedy person those who are thinking about me and my self I never tried it anyone people suffering from sadness ,I trying to get promoted people suffering from happiness and joy in your Life Time. Now in current situation in India and also world people are unemployed and have no many but our indian governor help to people to get free food from ration card , i also take part in leadership team ,i am Motivational speaker , Film script writer. There was my two dream firstly writer and secondly actor & also my own film is upcoming soon i done almost completely completed script for my film .I AM GOING TO SAY WORD OF HEART TOUCH OUT PLEASE READ IT" , firstly i thanks my father he supports me in this field they always getting inspired me by own his words and behavior ,they always said that he was a biggest person in the world in future and also they purchase fruit and chocolate for me in anytime & anyway , firstly my father buy him then call me Vivek you want a chocolate i will say yes papa but how many tell me ,papa: you tell me how much i buy him i told 1 or 2 chocolate but my father purchase whole the boxes of chocolate and they get suprised me. MY FATHER WAS BORN IN " 20 SEPTEMBER" 1971 IN INDIA.

1) MY FATHER FAVORITE CLOTHES IS KURTA PAIJMA AND ALSO STYLES SHOE

2) FAVORITE SINGER IS KISHORE DA

3) FAVORITE STATE GUJARAT AND KOLKATA , HIS VILLAGE IN BIHAR

4) FAVORITE COLOR BLACK AND WHITE

THEY ALSO LOVE cricket like IPL and one day t-20 .they also like watching a News daily and heard the song daily ,they also interested in tik tok video but in current time tik tok is banned in india but also few videos are in you tube. In lockdown time my family and me very enjoy day daily. my father play daily ludo with his sister and son, daughter.they always loved tea and coffee anytime call me . I make it tea for my father but some reason after the April to june they are suffering from fever and cough , weakness on 6 June 2020 my father death. they not told me say bye bye his life. After death of 6 June on 10 june my mom and dad anniversary.but my father is Best in the world they can do anything for me please take care of father and respect it of your parents.

ONE

· **James Anderson**

1. Short Biography Of James Anderson & Life Style, Career etc. During Writing This Book No Character, No Religion & No Caste Are Harmed. It's Only For Study Purpose. We don't want to hurt anyone.

James Anderson (born 30 July 1982) is an English international cricketer who plays for the England Test cricket team, and previously played for England's limited overs cricket teams. In domestic cricket, he represents Lancashire County Cricket Club.

Anderson made his Test debut in 2003, played for England's One-Day International (ODI) team between 2002 and 2015, and played for England's Twenty20 International (T20I) team between 2007 and 2009. On the occasion of England's 1,000th Test in 2018, Anderson was named in the country's greatest all-time Test XI by the England and Wales Cricket Board. As of December 2022, he is ranked as the number two Test bowler in the world in the ICC Men's Player Rankings.

Anderson plays as a right-arm fast-medium bowler. Among fast bowlers, he is the leading Test wicket-taker of all-time, being the only fast bowler to have taken 600 or more Test wickets, and is England's record Test wicket-taker. He has played the most Test matches for England, and the second-most of any cricketer, behind Sachin Tendulkar. He is also England's highest wicket-taker in ODIs with 269. He is regarded as one of the greatest swing bowlers in the history of cricket, and has taken over 1000 first-class wickets. As a batsman, he and Joe Root hold the world record for highest tenth-wicket stand in Tests (198).

· **James Anderson personal life**

James Anderson was a pupil at St Mary's and St Theodore's RC High School, Burnley. He played cricket at Burnley Cricket Club from a young age. His childhood dream was to be a cricketer, and at the age of 17, after a growth spurt, Anderson was one of the fastest bowlers in the Lancashire League. He stated that "I've always bowled seam, but when I was about 17 I don't know what it was but I just started bowling fast all of a sudden". He is a keen football fan who supports his local club Burnley.

Just months after his debut he had become one of the biggest stars in English cricket. Continuous alteration of hair styles, attractive looks, and up-to-the-minute outfits earned him comparisons with some of the most recognisable sports personalities around, including David Beckham. In 2006 he married Daniella Lloyd, a model he met in 2004 while on England duty in London; he stated that marriage has made him "a much happier person". The couple have two children.

Anderson has ventured into fashion design since 2012, designing for Elvis Jesus with proceeds of the sale going to his sponsored charity, Nordoff-Robbins. Anderson also agreed to be the face of British hair styling brand Hairbond in June 2013 In April 2014, he launched his first collection with London-based menswear brand, Chess London. He has stated that he would like to be "the first cricketer to become a designer". He launched his own menswear brand in late October 2014, and has been working in conjunction with British watchmaker Harold Pinchbeck to release a watch in 2015.

Anderson became the first cricketer to model naked for Attitude, "Britain's biggest-selling gay magazine", in September 2010. He stated "if there are any gay cricketers they should feel confident enough to come out because I don't think there is any homophobia in cricket."

· **James Anderson Domestic career**

Anderson made his competitive debut for the Lancashire Cricket Board in a List A one-day match against Suffolk in the 2000 NatWest Trophy, where he claimed the wicket of Russell Catley as his first competitive wicket. Anderson later made his first-class debut for Lancashire in 2002; he played 13 matches and took 50 wickets at an average of 22.28, including three five-wicket hauls. He took his maiden first-class wicket in May 2002, dismissing Ian Ward.He was awarded the NBC Denis Compton Award for Lancashire's most promising young County player in the 2002 season. In 2003, Anderson became the youngest player to take a hat-trick for Lancashire, just a week before his Test match debut against Zimbabwe; it was the first hat-trick at Old Trafford in eight years. In a match against Worcestershire in May 2004, Anderson recorded his maiden first-class ten-wicket haul.

2005 was Anderson's first full season for Lancashire. He was propelled into the England side soon after his Lancashire debut and had returned to rediscover his form after winter tours with England where he had spent most of his time on the sidelines, and when given a chance for England he often bowled poorly due to a lack of match practice. He finished the season with 60 first-class wickets at an average of 30.21 and 27 one day wickets at an average of 22.00.

Anderson was prevented from playing much for Lancashire in the 2006 season by a stress fracture of the back sustained in early May. He played in only two matches for Lancashire, and at one point it was considered sending Anderson to play for Glamorgan to prove his fitness; however, Lancashire decided they would rather have Anderson play for them if only in a limited capacity. In the only first-class match he played for Lancashire that season, he was limited to three four-over spells by the ECB who were wary of injuring him again.

In 2008, after the Test and One-Day series against South Africa ended at the beginning of September, Anderson was made unavailable to play for Lancashire for the rest of the season. He finished the season with 20 first-class wickets at 7.75 for Lancashire.At the start of the 2009 English cricket season, Anderson took career-best match figures in a first-class match with 11/109 against Sussex as Lancashire won by 8 wickets. It was the only first-class match he played for Lancashire before being called into the England squad for a series against the West Indies. As of 26 April 2009, Anderson had taken 188 wickets at 24.37 from 48 first-class matches with Lancashire, and 66 wickets at 21.78 in 44 list A matches.

· James Anderson International career

When Anderson was selected for the England one-day squad, he had played only five List A matches, taking 23 wickets at an average of 26.75. At the age of 20, he made his ODI debut on 15 December 2002 against Australia at Melbourne. He opened the bowling and recorded figures of 1/46 from six overs. His debut came before he was even awarded his County cap, which occurred in 2003. He showed good promise in this series – a three-team tournament also including Sri Lanka – which earned him a place in the 2003 World Cup squad. It was here that he really broke into international cricket with a match-winning spell against Pakistan, where he took four wickets in day/night game to collect the Man of the Match award. In what proved to be England's last match of the tournament he conceded 12 runs off the penultimate over against eventual world champions Australia, and England lost a closely fought contest.

In the summer of 2003, he made his first Test cricket appearance against Zimbabwe at Lord's, and took five wickets in an innings on debut, becoming the 42nd Englishman to do so. His success continued in the subsequent One-Day tournaments against Pakistan (against whom he took a hat-trick at The Oval), South Africa and Zimbabwe. His hat-trick against Pakistan, the first by an English bowler in an ODI, claimed the wickets of Abdul Razzaq, Shoaib Akhtar and Mohammad Sami.

The Test series against South Africa dented Anderson's reputation as England's golden boy in a series England drew 2–2 after coming from behind, Anderson finished the five-match series with 15 wickets at an average of 39.86. His best figures of 5/102 came at Trent Bridge in the third Test where he used movement of the seam to claim his second five-wicket haul in his fifth Test.

Although Anderson was England's lead wicket taker, Graeme Smith – the South African captain – particularly punished Anderson's bowling, taking 157 runs at a strike rate of 90.23 off his bowling in the series and only being dismissed once. In August, despite a mixed series against South Africa, Anderson was named Young Cricketer of the Year; he became the first player to be unanimously voted the award. In September, Anderson was awarded a central contract with the ECB. He suffered from a niggling knee injury and fatigue as the season wore on the knee injury – to a tendon on the outside of his left knee – meant he was rested for the winter tour of Bangladesh. After the South Africa series and some good performances by other bowlers during the Bangladesh tour, Anderson admitted that he was no longer an automatic choice for England.

Anderson has an unusual bowling action. At the moment of delivery he has his head down, eyes closed and does not look where he is bowling; he attempted to bowl with his head up but found that he lost pace in doing so, so reverted to his original action. In 2003, ex-England pace bowler Bob Willis claimed that Anderson would only be able to play for five years with his action. Between 2004 and 2005, the England coaching staff attempted to alter Anderson's bowling action. Anderson was selected in the One-Day and Test squads for the winter tour Sri Lanka, but injuries left him able to play in only one of the three Tests on that tour. He bowled well below his potential to collect figures of 0–85 in his sole appearance.

- **James Anderson in 2004–05: West Indies, Zimbabwe and Pakistan**

Although fit and included in both the Test and one-day squads for the tour of the West Indies, Anderson did not play in the Test series, having been superseded by players such as James Kirtley. He did feature in the ODI series which England drew 2–2, playing in 4 matches and taking 4 wickets at an average of 37.00 in the final match of the series, Anderson took his 50th ODI wicket, that of Chris Gayle for 41. After the ODI series against the West Indies, Anderson had 50 wickets from 31 ODIs at an average of 23.78.

Anderson retained his place in the Test squad, and his next big break came when an injury to Simon Jones forced the Welshman out of the last three Tests of the 2004 summer series against the West Indies. Despite being in the team, Anderson's bowling was used infrequently. It was clear now that Anderson had now not only lost all his form and rhythm, but consequentially all his confidence as well. A performance by a resurgent Anderson in the final Test of the summer prompted speculation that he had regained his confidence and would return to the top of his game.

He was selected for the winter tour to Zimbabwe and South Africa. Much of the post-season talk, however, was dominated by the debate over whether to go on tour to Zimbabwe. England eventually did end up in Harare, after a brief stop over in Namibia. Anderson once again struggled in his three One-Day appearances. The England management, however, continued to show faith in his ability.

Travelling as a barely-used reserve on the winter South Africa tour while seemingly struggling for form, Anderson was given another shot at redemption, after Simon Jones was dropped for the third Test after a poor performance in the second. Anderson, though, did even worse than Jones, collecting figures of 2/117 and 0/32 in his two innings. Anderson spent the following summer with Lancashire; bowling regularly a quota of overs one would associate with a new ball bowler, something he had not done enough in his England stint. He was recalled to the England squad for the last match of the 2005 Ashes series after taking 60 wickets for Lancashire in 2005, once again as a replacement for the injured Jones, but all-rounder Paul Collingwood was selected for the team.

Anderson was selected in the Test squad for the tour of Pakistan, but spinner Shaun Udal was chosen to fill the bowler's spot left empty by the still injured Simon Jones. When Ashley Giles had to miss the third Test due to injury, young Durham debutant seamer Liam Plunkett was chosen ahead of Anderson and Anderson did not play a single Test on the tour. Despite this disappointment he played in all five of England's One-Day games in Pakistan, showing improvements in form to be England's joint-leading wicket-taker in the series with Andrew Flintoff, taking 7 wickets at 25.57.

· **James Anderson in 2006: India and Australia**

Anderson was not selected for the senior side's tour to India in January 2006 as Simon Jones returned from injury and was chosen ahead of him. Instead, Anderson was selected for England A's tour of the West Indies. In February, days before the start of the first A-match between England and the West Indies, James Anderson (along with batsmen Alastair Cook and Owais Shah) was called up as an injury reinforcement to the England senior squad in India, after captain Michael Vaughan and fast bowler Simon Jones flew home with knee injuries and vice-captain Marcus

Trescothick departed for undisclosed "personal" reasons. After an unconvincing display by Liam Plunkett in the second Test in Mohali Anderson was recalled for the final match of the series. He impressed in England's victory, taking figures of 4/40 in the first innings.

After his impressive display in the final match in India, Anderson looked likely to feature as one of England's main bowlers in both the ODI series and Test matches against Pakistan and Sri Lanka; however an early season stress fracture of the back ruled Anderson out for all of the summer internationals and all but two matches of his county season. Lancashire teammate Sajid Mahmood was called up to the England squad the replacement for Anderson.

Anderson was named in England's Champions Trophy and Ashes squads in September 2006 although at that point he had not played any first-class cricket in six months.He was straight back into England colours for the 0–5 Ashes whitewash against Australia. His performance, like much of the England team, was well below standard. Anderson was sent home midway through the One-Day tournament with Australia and New Zealand as a precaution when he felt a twinge in his back during the tournament he had begun to regain some of his form and in the four matches he played he took 8 wickets at an average of 20.62.

· James Anderson in 2007: World Cup

Although Anderson was returned home early from the England's victorious ODI series in Australia, Anderson was selected in England's squad for the 2007 Cricket World Cup. He recovered from his back injury and was expected to play ahead of the likes of Liam Plunkett, Sajid Mahmood and

Jon Lewis. However, on 14 March 2007, only days before England's first game, it was reported by the BBC that Anderson had broken his finger during fielding practice and his involvement in the tournament was in question, although he was able to play despite the pain.

· James Anderson in 2007: West Indies, India and Sri Lanka

When Peter Moores replaced Duncan Fletcher as England coach after the World Cup, it was felt that Anderson would benefit under new management; along with the rest of the England team he was allowed to play more for his county. It was felt that it was not beneficial for players who were not representing England to just sit on the sideline and match practice would allow him to rediscover his form. Anderson did not feature in the Test series against the West Indies, but he did play in the ODI series. During the second ODI, he clashed with Runako Morton when he appeared to get in the way of Morton when the batsman was running between the wickets. Anderson was fined half of his match fee for the incident and match referee Mike Procter stated "James Anderson is not a player with a reputation for bad behaviour...and I am sure he will do everything he can to ensure there is no repeat of this unfortunate incident". Anderson finished the series with five wickets at 30.40 as England lost the series 2–1.Anderson bowling during the second Test of India's tour of England in 2007. He opened the bowling with Ryan Sidebottom.

Anderson played in all three Tests of the series with India, coming into the side for the injured Matthew Hoggard and leading a pace attack comprising himself, Ryan Sidebottom and Chris Tremlett with only 20 caps between them. In the first Test of the series, Anderson claimed his 50th Test wicket when he dismissed Mahendra Singh Dhoni for 0. the feat was achieved in Anderson's 17th Test match and after the match he had 53 wickets at an average of 35.67.

He became the first England bowler to dismiss Rahul Dravid, Sachin Tendulkar, and Sourav Ganguly in the same innings. Although England lost the series, Anderson demonstrated greater consistency than before and managed 14 wickets, at 35.57 and getting the Man of the Series award.He also managed to get his name on the honours board at Lord's for the second time with his best Test figures of 5/42. The ODI series which followed was England's first ODI series win at home in three years. Anderson was the leading wicket-taker of either side with 14 wickets at an average of 22.57.

In the first ODI of the series, Anderson claimed his 100th ODI wicket when he dismissed Gautam Gambhir for 3 after the match, he had taken 103 wickets from 70 matches at an average of 27.02. Anderson was also included for the England squad for the World Twenty20, held in September 2007, replacing an injured Ravi Bopara. He played in all four of England's matches, taking three wickets at 34.00, as England failed to progress beyond the second stage of the competition. Following a successful summer, he was one of twelve players awarded a central contract for 2007/08 by the ECB.

Anderson was part of the squad which toured Sri Lanka in the winter. The One-Day side completed their first ever series victory in Sri Lanka; Anderson's contribution was four wickets in five matches at an average of 48.25 and tying down Sri Lanka's top order along with Sidebottom and Stuart Broad, although they finished with more wickets at a lower average. Despite suffering a bruised left ankle,Anderson was selected for the first Test. Although he bowled economically in the first innings, he was expensive in the second; during the course of the second innings he became only the second bowler in Test cricket to have six boundaries taken off a single over. He finished the match with figures of two wickets for 167 runs and was dropped for the final two Tests; his replacement was debutant Stuart Broad.

· James Anderson in 2008: New Zealand, South Africa and India

In the spring of 2008, Anderson toured New Zealand with England. He played in the Twenty20 series, which England won 2–0, and he was then involved in the one-day series which New Zealand won 3–2. Although he played in all five matches of the One-Day series, he struggled and only managed four wickets at an average of 67.50. In an effort to regain some form, Anderson was allowed to join Auckland Cricket Club, who were lacking their strike bowlers due to international call ups, as an overseas player.

The move was controversial with critics including Gavin Larsen, Wellington Cricket Club's chief executive, who feared that Anderson would be able to bowl himself into form. Although he was left out for the first Test, Anderson was recalled for the second when he and Stuart Broad replaced the out of form Steve Harmison and Matthew Hoggard after England were defeated by 189 runs; the decision to axe both bowlers was heralded as the end of an era in English cricket.

Anderson's selection was a surprise as it was expected that Broad would replace Harmison, but not that Hoggard would be dropped. In the first innings of the second Test, Anderson took 5/73 and finished with match figures of 7/130 and helped England to a 126-run victory. He sustained an ankle injury while playing football before the third Test but recovered in time to be selected. Anderson's performance in the final Test was less effective, recording match figures of 1/153 as England won the match by 121 runs and the series 2–1. Searching for consistency, Anderson's action reverted to the action he used in 2003, one with which he felt comfortable.

· **Anderson bowling against New Zealand in England**

He was retained for the home series, when New Zealand toured England later in 2008. He continued to enjoy success against the touring side, taking 19 wickets at 19.31 and finishing as the leading wicket-taker of the series. This was his highest return of wickets in a series. Anderson bowled well in the first Test, recording match figures of 130/5 as the match was drawn. In the second Test, Anderson finished with match figures of 5/139 as England won by six wickets; on the first day he struck New Zealand batsman Daniel Flynn in the face, knocking out a tooth, in a spell of short, aggressive bowling when he also hit Jacob Oram on the helmet. Anderson was disconcerted by injuring Flynn said that striking him "wasn't pleasant". In the final match of the series Anderson scored a career Test best of 28 in a partnership of 76 with Stuart Broad.

This was followed up by career best bowling of 7/43 in the first innings and Test best match figures of 9/98 overall as he won the Man of the Match award and England secured an innings and nine run victory and a 2–0 series win. Anderson's performance in the series prompted

England bowling coach Ottis Gibson to say that Anderson has the potential to become a world-class bowler if he can improve his self-belief. In the One-Day series that followed Anderson managed five wickets from five matches at an average of 41.40 as England lost the series 3–1.

After the Test series against New Zealand, Anderson's figures revealed that he struggled to bowl to left-handed batsmen and his contrasting fortunes between the start of his career and his resurgence. By the end of June 2008, Anderson had played 25 Test matches; in the 16 Tests before July 2007 he took 46 wickets at an average of 38.39, but since then in 9 Tests he took 43 wickets at 30.58 at a much lower strike rate. In the five Tests Anderson played against New Zealand in a four-month period, 22 of the 27 wickets he managed were against right-handed batsmen. Against the right-handers he averaged 20.77 compared to 38.60 against left-handers. This was an improvement however on his career statistics, since he averaged 70 wickets at 29.11 against right-handers and 19 at 54.94 against left-handers. This first became clear in the 2003 Test series against South Africa when Graeme Smith and Gary Kirsten milked him for 276 runs while only being dismissed once between them.

Anderson's batting showed a marked improvement in the summer's home Test series against South Africa. In the second innings of the second Test, at Headingley, Anderson scored a Test-career best 34 runs, having come to the crease as a nightwatchman late on Day 3. In the course of his innings he was struck on the wrist and then on the grille of his helmet by Dale Steyn. In the final match of the series, Anderson took his 100th Test wicket. The landmark wicket was that of Jacques Kallis Leg Before Wicket for 2 this feat was achieved in Anderson's 29th Test and after the match he had 104 wickets at an average of 34.51.

England's One-Day series in India was cut short due to terror attacks in Mumbai. Seven matches were due to be played, but due to the terrorism England flew home after five games. They were 5–0 down in the series and Anderson had not taken one wicket, despite bowling in every one of the five games.

· James Anderson in 2009: West Indies

Following the sacking of Peter Moores in January 2009, and the replacement of Kevin Pietersen by Andrew Strauss as England captain, England left for a tour to the West Indies.

Following two low-key performances in the warm-up matches against a St. Kitts XI and West Indies A, Anderson was dropped for the first Test in Jamaica. Surprisingly, the West Indies inflicted a large defeat on England, following a third innings batting collapse. With the form of Ryan Sidebottom a cause for concern, and some doubts over his fitness, Anderson was recalled for the second Test at the Sir Vivian Richards Stadium in Antigua. However, this match was abandoned with fewer than two overs bowled due to an unfit outfield. The Test match was rearranged to take place two days later at the Antigua Recreation Ground. After making 4 as a night-watchman during England's first innings, Anderson bowled 19 wicketless overs as the West Indies were bowled out for 285, although he did take the catch of Chris Gayle off Steve Harmison. After making 20, again as night-watchman, in the second batting innings, England fell one wicket short of bowling the West Indies out and securing a Test victory as the tail-enders of Daren Powell and Fidel Edwards survived 10 overs to bat out the draw.

After sitting out the tour match against the BCA President's XI in Barbados, England and the West Indies played the fourth Test at the Kensington Oval. Both sides found bowling difficult on a very flat track, and the first two innings produced 1,349 runs for the loss of just 15 wickets. England batted first and made 600/6 declared, and Anderson again opened the bowling in the West Indies reply. After striking early to dismiss Chris Gayle LBW on a referral, he also dismissed Shivnarine Chanderpaul and Sulieman Benn, finishing with 3 for 125 from 37 overs. With England batting out the match, Anderson did not feature again as the Test match was drawn.

With England still 1–0 down in a series they were expected by many to win comfortably, victory was needed in the fifth and final Test at Queen's Park Oval in Trinidad. After England made 546/6 declared, Anderson again struggled as the West Indies were bowled out for 544, a deficit of 2 runs, with Anderson picking up the wicket of wicket-keeper Dinesh Ramdin for 70 runs, with an economy of just 2.18, one of his best in Test cricket. With England setting the West Indies a target of 240 runs to win, Anderson had arguably his best innings of the tour. After dismissing opener Lendl Simmons, Anderson bowled 16 overs of reverse swing, picking up two more wickets as again England fell just short of victory, this time by two wickets.

With the Test series lost, England were keen to regain some honour in the T20 and ODIs which remained. After taking 3 for 48 in 8 overs in a warm-up match against the WIPA President's Select XI, Anderson led the England attack in the T20 international. Despite finishing with decent figures of 1–19 in 3 overs, England were beaten soundly. The first One-Day International, however, saw England inflict their first defeat on the West Indies of the tour. After posting 270 for 7 in their 50 overs, Rain interrupted the West Indies' reply, leading to the result being decided on the Duckworth–Lewis method. With the light fading, Anderson succeeded in having Kieron Pollard caught on the boundary by Steve Harmison. Due to the intricacies of the D/L system, this wicket ensured England won the match by a single run.

In the next two ODIs, England suffered two more defeats, with Anderson taking 3 for 37 from 9 overs in the second ODI, as well as making 8 with the bat,and went on to take 1 for 39 from 5 overs and 0 not out as England fell 2–1 behind in the five-match series. England therefore needed to win the fourth ODI in Barbados to keep the series alive. Bowling first, England restricted the West Indies to 239/9 in their 50 overs, with Anderson himself taking the wicket of Fidel Edwards to finish with figures of 1 for 41 with 1 maiden in the 10 he bowled. Duckworth-Lewis again helped England as they chased down 136 in 18 overs to win by nine wickets.

Thus, the series was tied at 2–2 going into the final match in St. Lucia. The West Indies won the toss and elected to bowl first, with England able to post 172/5 in 29 overs (the innings shortened by rain). With 29 overs to chase 173 for victory, the West Indies lost Gayle to Anderson in the first over with the score at 1/1, Anderson going on to add the wicket of Kieron Pollard as he finished with match figures of 2/34 from 6 overs as England won the match by 26 runs, with Anderson's Lancashire teammate Andrew Flintoff taking a hat-trick.

Anderson finished the tour with 9 wickets at an average of 38.00 from the Test series, with an economy rate of 2.65

runs per over from both innings and best match figures coming in the fifth Test at Trinidad, as well as accumulating 24 runs at an average of 12.00, with a highest-score of 20. In the ODIs, Anderson took 9 wickets at 21.11 and an economy rate of 5.00 runs per over and 8 runs at an equivalent average. He then rejected offers to play in the IPL since he wanted to commit to a bright future for England over the following summer.The Wisden Trophy was up for grabs again a few months later when the West Indies replaced Zimbabwe, who were still excluded from participating in Test match cricket by the ICC (although originally the tour had been scheduled to be played by Sri Lanka, who pulled out to allow their players to play in the IPL), in a two-Test and three-ODI tour. Anderson was selected after a bright start to the season with Lancashire, which included figures of 11–109 in a match against Sussex at Hove.

The first Test was held at Lord's, beginning on 6 May 2020. Anderson was not involved directly until the second day, with England batting first, but made only a single in a 19-ball innings. With the wicket showing a green tinge and some cloud cover, Anderson was expected to excel. However he struggled to find his length bowling in the first innings and finished wicketless from seven overs having conceded 32. An improvement in the second innings saw him take the first two wickets after the follow-on, including that of the West Indies captain Chris Gayle, and finishing with figures of 2–38 from 15 overs and match figures of 2–70 as England won by ten wickets.

From Lord's, the teams moved to Chester-le-Street for the second and final Test of the series. England again won the toss and chose to bat, and proceeded to dominate the West Indies bowling attack, amassing 569–6 declared. Anderson was sent in at the end of the first day in his role as night-watchman to protect Pietersen. Batting with Alastair Cook, they made a partnership of 44, Anderson hitting 14 of them to extend his run of innings without a duck in Test cricket. Later on day three, he was given the ball as England set out to take 20 West Indian wickets and secure match victory. Anderson found some significant swing in the cloudy conditions there, and proceeded to skittle through the West Indies top order, taking the first three wickets (including Gayle again) leaving the West Indies on 68/3.

Two late strikes secured Anderson a five-wicket haul, his first in 19 innings since his 7-wicket haul against New Zealand at Trent Bridge the previous summer. Anderson went on to take 4 further wickets after the West Indies were asked to follow-on (for the second time in the series) and England went on to win by an innings and 83 runs. With nine wickets in the match for 125 runs, Anderson was named the Man of the Match, only the second time in his career he had achieved this in a Test match.

· **Anderson bowling at Edgbaston during the 2009 Ashes**

The first match of the following ODI series at Headingley was abandoned due to heavy rain, leaving two One-Day matches to be played. Anderson was named in the England squad for the series, and was selected for both matches. In the first match at Bristol, he bowled six overs for nineteen, with one maiden, but finished wicketless as the West Indies were bowled out for 160. England went on to win the match by six wickets, meaning Anderson was not needed to bat. Neither was he required to bat in the last match of the tour as England scored 328/7 from their 50 overs. Although Anderson went at a run a ball in reply, conceding 58 from 9.4 overs, he took three wickets including the last of the match (that of Sulieman Benn) as the West Indies fell 58 runs short, sealing a 2–0 victory for England in both the Test and ODI series.

· James Anderson in 2009–10: South Africa

Anderson went on the tour of South Africa as one of the leaders of the English attack, having established himself in all formats of the game. In the opening T20 International, Anderson failed to pick up a wicket, although he was fairly economical, going at 8 runs an over. Anderson improved in the following match, bowling 4 for 28 runs, picking up a wicket. He was the pick of the English bowlers as South Africa won the match, posting over 200. Anderson bowled well in the ODI series, picking up regular wickets. He claimed 3–60 in the second ODI, and 5–23 in the fourth match. The four-match Test series was drawn 1–1, with Anderson bowling well. He picked up 5 wickets for 63 runs during the 3rd Test, as well as 4–73 in the opening match.

· James Anderson in 2010: Bangladesh and Pakistan

Anderson was selected in the England squad for the 2010 T20 World Cup, despite not being regarded as a specialist in this format of cricket. He did not play in the opening group match against the West Indies. With England playing well in the tournament, and with the three-man seam attack of Stuart Broad, Ryan Sidebottom and Tim Bresnan performing, Anderson could not break into the side. England went on to win the tournament, beating Australia in the final.

England faced Bangladesh in a two-match Test series. England were expected to win easily and cruised to victory in the first Test, with Anderson taking figures of 4–78 and 1–84. Anderson also played in the second Test, finishing with figures of 1–45 and 3–16. England won the series 2–0. Anderson played in the first ODI, but was expensive, taking figures of 3–74. He was wicketless in the second game as England suffered a shock defeat. Anderson did not play in the decider, which England won to take the series.

England then played Pakistan at home. It was during this series that Anderson established himself as one of the world's best Test bowlers. In the first match he took 5–54 and 6–17 which England won. This left Anderson with match figures of 11–71. He helped England win the second Test, achieving figures of 4–20 in the first innings. Anderson continued to impress in the final two Tests continuing to be economical and providing a wicket-taking threat. Anderson was rested for the first ODI, but returned in the second, taking 1–36 in ten overs. He then took 3–26 in the third match, before playing the remaining matches of the series. Although Anderson struggled to take wickets, his economical bowling frustrated the opposition and kept the run rate down. By the end of the tour, Anderson had established himself as the leader of the England attack, with his swing bowling making him one of the most feared bowlers in the world.

· **James Anderson in 2010–11: Australia**

As expected, Anderson was selected in the England squad to play Australia, where he developed his own wobble-seam delivery to combat the Kookaburra ball that doesn't swing as much for as long. Anderson played well in the opening tour games and took two wickets in the opening Test match, which finished as a draw. In the second

Test England thrashed Australia, winning by an innings and 71 runs. Anderson took 4–51 in the first innings and Australia were never able to recover. England lost the third Test, but Anderson still impressed taking 4 wickets. Anderson took 4–44 in the fourth Test, which England won to retain the Ashes. He then took 4–66 and 3–61 as England won the fifth Test and series 3–1. During the series Anderson became the second youngest England bowler to claim 200 Test wickets. Anderson was rested at the start of the ODI series, but with England struggling he was recalled, taking 2–57 in the third match. In the sixth match Anderson took 1–91 of his ten overs as the England team struggled. Anderson took 3–48 in the final match of the series, but it wasn't enough to prevent another defeat as England lost the one-day series 6–1.

· **James Anderson in 2011: World Cup, Sri Lanka and India**

Anderson was selected in the squad for the 2011 World Cup and played in the opening game against the Netherlands. He was involved in the dramatic tie against India, where both teams posted 338, and also played as England suffered an embarrassing defeat against Ireland. His best match of the tournament came when he helped England defend 171 against South Africa, where he bowled six overs, collecting figures of 2–16. He was left out of the team against the West Indies, which England won. Anderson did not appear in England's final match against Sri Lanka, in which they lost by ten wickets and so bowed out at the quarter-final stage of the competition. Overall, Anderson had a disappointing tournament, although the pitches did not suit his style of bowling being unable to get the ball to swing.

Anderson was part of the England team when Sri Lanka toured in 2011. Anderson took 3–66 in the first innings, but was unable to bowl in the second due to an injury. England won the first Test after Sri Lanka collapsed for 82 all out in the second innings. Anderson was ruled out of the second Test through injury but returned for the third, taking figures of 2–56 and 2–81 as England drew the match, but won the series 1–0. Anderson took 4–18 in the first ODI but was wicketless in the second match. In the fourth match he returned to his best, taking 3–24. In the final match he took 2–55, helping England to a series win.

England's next opponents were India. England needed to win the four match series by two games to overtake India in the world rankings and become the new top-ranked Test team. Anderson shone in the first Test, taking 5–65 as England took a 1–0 lead. Anderson took 5 more wickets in the second Test and a further 6 in the third as England took a 3–0 series lead. Anderson took 3 more wickets in the final Test as England won the series 4–0 and became the new world Number Ones. Following Anderson's performance, he was widely considered the premier fast bowler in the world. Anderson took 3–48 in the third ODI but was left out of the final game of the series as had already won, taking a 2–0 lead into the final match, which they also won by 6 wickets.

- **James Anderson in 2011–12: Pakistan and Sri Lanka**

England toured Pakistan at the back end of 2012. The series was held in the UAE. England struggled in the conditions and slumped to a heavy defeat in the first Test, with Anderson largely ineffectual. England again lost the second Test, with poor performances from the batsmen giving the bowlers little to work with. Anderson took his best figures of the tour, 3–35 in the final match of the series, but it wasn't enough to prevent a whitewash for Pakistan. After the series, England moved on to Sri Lanka for a two-match Test series. Anderson took 5–72 in the first innings but it wasn't enough to prevent a fourth straight defeat for England. Anderson was praised for his performance in conditions which did not favour seam bowlers. England won the final Test to level the series, with Anderson taking figures of 4–98 in the match. As a result of his performances, Anderson was named England Cricketer of the Year.

· James Anderson in 2012: West Indies and South Africa

In the second Test against West Indies, Anderson took 4–43 at Trent Bridge, a ground where he always performed due to the swing-friendly conditions. With England taking a 2–0 series lead, Anderson was rested for the final match of the series to help him avoid burnout. Anderson played in the ODI series against the West Indies, taking 2–38 in the second match. England then played Australia in 5 ODIs. Anderson took 2–55 in the first match, and 2–34 in the fourth match. There were suggestions that Anderson would play no part in the series, both to rest him and to deprive Australia of facing him ahead of the Ashes series the following year. However, despite this, Anderson played a key part in the series.

England faced South Africa at the end of the summer, with their Number One ranking on the line. The series was also anticipated as a chance to see Anderson go head to head with Dale Steyn, regarded as the world's two best seam bowlers. The series was a disappointment for England. They lost the first Test by an innings, with Anderson managing figures of 1–116. The second Test was a tighter affair, with the match ending in a draw, but Anderson could only manage three wickets in the match. England lost the third Test, meaning a 2–0 series defeat, and South Africa earned their place at the top of the Test rankings. Anderson took 4–44 in the third ODI, and 2–41 in the fifth as the series ended as 2–2 draw. This was seen as a positive result for England, with several young players being blooded against an experienced South African team.

- **James Anderson in 2012–13: India, New Zealand and Champions Trophy**

Following the defeat to South Africa, Andrew Strauss retired and was replaced as captain by Alistair Cook. The first series under the leadership of Cook was against India. England lost the first Test by 9 wickets, with Anderson taking just one wicket in the match. England won the second Test convincingly, but Anderson again struggled in conditions more suited to spinners. Anderson performed much better in the third Test, taking six wickets overall. Anderson took the wicket of Sachin Tendulkar in the 1st innings of the third Test to equal Muttiah Muralitharan as the most successful bowler against Tendulkar with a total of eight dismissals. With England needing just a draw to win the series in the final Test, Anderson took 4–81 to help England draw the match and win the series 2–1.

In the tour of New Zealand, Anderson returned to the ODI side. In February 2013 during England's loss of the 1st One day international in New Zealand, with the wicket of BJ Watling, his 529th in international cricket, Anderson overtook Ian Botham to become England's all-time highest wicket-taker. He took 5–34 in the second match as England went on to win the series. Anderson took 4–137 in the first Test and went on to take wickets in every innings in the series. The series itself finished 0–0, with the batsmen dominating on good batting wickets.Anderson bowling during the Champions Trophy match in which he became England's leading wicket-taker in ODIs.Anderson played a key role in the 2013 Champions Trophy. He took 3–30 against Australia as England made a winning start to their campaign. During the match ICC Champions Trophy match against Australia he became England's leading ODI wicket-taker when he took his 235th wicket. In the final Group A match he took 3–32 as England reached the semi-finals of the competition. England shocked South Africa and won by 7 wickets, with Anderson taking 2–14 off 8 overs. England played India, the favourites for the competition in the final, in what proved to be a rain interrupted match. Only being able to bowl four overs, Anderson took 1–24, but a poor batting performance meant that England lost the match and India went on to become champions.

In the opening match of the Test series against New Zealand, Anderson took match figures of 7–70. On the second day of the 1st Test against New Zealand, he became the fourth English bowler to take 300 Test wickets when he dismissed Peter Fulton. England went on to win the series 2–0. Anderson took 3–31 in the first ODI, and also played in the second match. England lost the series 2–1.

• James Anderson in 2015: World Cup

Anderson failed to take a wicket in the first match against Australia, finishing with figures of 0–67. In the next match against New Zealand he finished with figures of 0–37 as England suffered a humiliating eight wicket defeat. He took his first wickets of the tournament against Scotland as he collected figures of 2–30 as England won their first game of the tournament. He was again wicket less in England's defeat to Sri Lanka. In their must win game against Bangladesh, Anderson took figures of 2–45 but was later the last man out as England lost the game to exit the World Cup. In their final group game against Afghanistan, Anderson bowled economically, finishing with figures of 1–18 as England won their final match of the tournament.

- **James Anderson in 2015: Australia**

In the first Test Anderson took figures of 3–43 in Australia's first innings to help restrict them to 308, and England went on to win the game by 169 runs. In the second Test he failed to take a wicket in the whole match, finishing with figures of 0–99 in the first innings and 0–48 in the second innings as Australia won the match by 405 runs. In the third Test, Anderson took 6–47 in the Australian first innings to help restrict them to 136. He took 1–15 in the second innings but injured himself in the process. Although England won the game to go 2–1 up in the series, Anderson was ruled out of the remainder of the series through injury. England went on to win the series 3–2.

- **James Anderson in 2015: Pakistan**

Anderson recovered from his injury in time for the Test series against Pakistan. In the first innings of the first Test, Anderson took figures of 2–42 and bowled economically as Pakistan were dismissed for 523. In the second innings he took figures of 2–30 as Pakistan were bowled out for 173, but England did not have enough time to force a win and the match finished in a draw. In the second Test Anderson took 1–40 in the first innings, before finishing with figures of 2–22 in Pakistan's second innings as they were dismissed for 354. However, England's batting was unable to chase down the target and the suffered a 127 run defeat. England needed to win the final Test of the series to level it, and Pakistan were dismissed cheaply for 234 in the first innings, with Anderson taking 4–17. However, they recovered in their second innings, scoring 355, despite Anderson taking 2–52. An England second innings collapse saw Pakistan win the series 2–0.

· James Anderson in 2018: Pakistan and India

Anderson was selected in the England squad to face Pakistan in May 2018 in a two Test match series. In the first Test match, which Pakistan won, Anderson had team leading match figures of 4–94. In the second Test he took 5 wickets at the expense of 78 runs, to help England win by an innings and 55 runs. Overall Anderson took a team leading 9 wickets during the series, with the series being tied 1–1.

Anderson was in the side as England played their 1,000[th] Test match, during the first Test against India at Edgbaston in the five-match series. During the second Test, Anderson picked up his 100th wicket at Lord's in Tests, and his 550th Test match wicket as he took 5–20 in the first innings, and finished with match figures of 9–43. The third Test at Trent Bridge was won by India as they recovered from a 2–0 start to the series, Anderson took his 100th wicket against India in Tests. In the fifth Test, Anderson equalled Glenn McGrath's record for the most Test wickets by a pace bowler (563), he then surpassed this later in the game when he took his 564th Test wicket. Anderson took 24 wickets at an average of 18.13 during the series, the most wickets by any bowler during the series as England beat India 4–1.

• James Anderson in 2018–19: Sri Lanka and West Indies

Anderson played the first two Tests of the three-match series in Sri Lanka. In the first Test, he took match figures of 1/53 from 22 overs, helping England to their first ever Test win in Galle. The second Test saw a record breaking 38 wickets taken by spin bowlers, with Anderson going wicketless for the first time in almost two years. Anderson was rested for the third Test, to allow Stuart Broad match practice. This meant Anderson finished with just 1 wicket in the series, the lowest in a Test series he had participated in since 2003.

Anderson took a five-wicket haul during the first innings of the three-match Test series against the West Indies at Kensington Oval, Barbados. This was his 27th five-wicket haul, tying Ian Botham's record for England in Test matches. Whilst en route to his five-wicket haul, he also became the first English bowler to take 200 Test wickets away from home. Despite this, England lost the match by 381 runs, the West Indies' largest victory in terms of runs at home. Anderson finished the series, which England lost 2–1, with 10 wickets at an average of 24.50.

• James Anderson in 2020: West Indies and Pakistan

On 29 May 2020, Anderson was named in a 55-man group of players to begin training ahead of international fixtures starting in England following the COVID-19 pandemic. On 17 June 2020, Anderson was included in England's 30-man squad to start training behind closed doors for the Test series against the West Indies. On 4 July 2020, Anderson was named in England's thirteen-man squad for the first Test match of the series. On 25 August, Anderson became the first fast bowler to reach 600 Test wickets.In November 2020, Anderson was nominated for the ICC Men's Test Cricketer of the Decade award.

- **James Anderson Achievements**

On 25 July 2016, during the second Test of that year's England-Pakistan series at Old Trafford, he became the first fast bowler to take 50 wickets against all other 7 major Test-playing nations, Australia, India, New Zealand, Pakistan, South Africa, Sri Lanka and West Indies. In December 2019, in the first Test against South Africa, Anderson became the ninth cricketer to play in 150 Test matches. In January 2020, in the second Test of the series against South Africa, Anderson took his 28th five-wicket haul in Test cricket. He surpassed Sir Ian Botham's record of 27, to become the bowler with the most five-wicket hauls for England in Test cricket.

He is the only seam bowler to take 300+ Test wickets on home soil. He is the first pace bowler, and second player overall, to take 100 Test wickets at a single venue (at Lord's; Muttiah Muralitharan has taken 100 wickets at three separate grounds in Sri Lanka) He has the most international Test deliveries bowled by a pace bowler.He holds the world record for "not out" batting performances in Test cricket, achieving his 62nd Test "not out" at Lord's in 2017, passing the previous record of 61 set by Courtney Walsh.

On 5 July 2021, playing for Lancashire against Kent in the LV= County Championship, Anderson took seven wickets for 19 runs (including 5 maiden overs), a new First Class best. It also meant he passed 1,000 First Class wickets.On 18 December 2021, Anderson during England's 1st innings in the 2nd Test of the Ashes, became the first-ever batsman to remain not out in Test cricket on 100 instances.

- **James Anderson Awards**

On 8 December 2011, he was awarded the Freedom of the Borough of Burnley. In the 2015 Queen's Birthday Honours, Anderson was appointed an Officer of the Order of the British Empire "for services to cricket". On 11 February 2016, he received his OBE at Buckingham Palace.

TWO

LET'S KNOW ABOUT CRICKET

· Let's Know About Cricket

Cricket is a bat-and-ball game played between two teams of eleven players on a field at the centre of which is a 22-yard (20-metre) pitch with a wicket at each end, each comprising two bails balanced on three stumps. The game proceeds when a player on the fielding team, called the bowler, "bowls" (propels) the ball from one end of the pitch towards the wicket at the other end. The batting side's players score runs by striking the bowled ball with a bat and running between the wickets, while the bowling side tries to prevent this by keeping the ball within the field and getting it to either wicket, and dismiss each batter (so they are "out"). Means of dismissal include being bowled, when the ball hits the stumps and dislodges the bails, and by the fielding side either catching a hit ball before it touches the ground, or hitting a wicket with the ball before a batter can cross the crease line in front of the wicket to complete a run. When ten batters have been dismissed, the innings ends and the teams swap roles. The game is adjudicated by two umpires, aided by a third umpire and match referee in international matches.

Forms of cricket range from Twenty20, with each team batting for a single innings of 20 overs and the game generally lasting three hours, to Test matches played over five days. Traditionally cricketers play in all-white kit, but in limited overs cricket they wear club or team colours. In addition to the basic kit, some players wear protective gear to prevent injury caused by the ball, which is a hard, solid spheroid made of compressed leather with a slightly raised sewn seam enclosing a cork core layered with tightly wound string.

The earliest reference to cricket is in South East England in the mid-16th century. It spread globally with the expansion of the British Empire, with the first international matches in the second half of the 19th century. The game's governing body is the International Cricket Council (ICC), which has over 100 members, twelve of which are full members who play Test matches. The game's rules, the Laws of Cricket, are maintained by Marylebone Cricket Club (MCC) in London. The sport is followed primarily in South Asia, Australasia, the United Kingdom, southern Africa and the West Indies.Women's cricket, which is organised and played separately, has also achieved international standard. The most successful side playing international cricket is Australia, which has won seven One Day International trophies, including five World Cups, more than any other country and has been the top-rated Test side more than any other country.

- **History of cricket to 1725**

Cricket is one of many games in the "club ball" sphere that basically involve hitting a ball with a hand-held implement; others include baseball (which shares many similarities with cricket, both belonging in the more specific bat-and-ball games category), golf, hockey, tennis, squash, badminton and table tennis. In cricket's case, a key difference is the existence of a solid target structure, the wicket (originally, it is thought, a "wicket gate" through which sheep were herded), that the batter must defend. The cricket historian Harry Altham identified three "groups" of "club ball" games: the "hockey group", in which the ball is driven to and fro between two targets (the goals); the "golf group", in which the ball is driven towards an undefended target (the hole); and the "cricket group", in which "the ball is aimed at a mark (the wicket) and driven away from it".

It is generally believed that cricket originated as a children's game in the south-eastern counties of England, sometime during the medieval period.Although there are claims for prior dates, the earliest definite reference to cricket being played comes from evidence given at a court case in Guildford in January 1597 (Old Style), equating to January 1598 in the modern calendar. The case concerned ownership of a certain plot of land and the court heard the testimony of a 59-year-old coroner, John Derrick, who gave witness that.

Being a scholler in the ffree schoole of Guldeford hee and diverse of his fellows did runne and play there at creckett and other plaies.

Given Derrick's age, it was about half a century earlier when he was at school and so it is certain that cricket was being played c. 1550 by boys in Surrey. The view that it was originally a children's game is reinforced by Randle Cotgrave's 1611 English-French dictionary in which he defined the noun "crosse" as "the crooked staff wherewith boys play at cricket" and the verb form "crosser" as "to play at cricket".

One possible source for the sport's name is the Old English word "cryce" (or "cricc") meaning a crutch or staff. In Samuel Johnson's Dictionary, he derived cricket from "cryce, Saxon, a stick". In Old French, the word "criquet" seems to have meant a kind of club or stick. Given the strong medieval trade connections between south-east England and the County of Flanders when the latter belonged to the Duchy of Burgundy, the name may have been derived from the Middle Dutch (in use in Flanders at the time) "krick"(-e), meaning a stick (crook). Another possible source is the Middle Dutch word "krickstoel", meaning a long low stool used for kneeling in church and which resembled the long low wicket with two stumps used in early cricket. According to Heiner Gillmeister, a European language expert of Bonn University, "cricket" derives from the Middle Dutch phrase for hockey, met de (krik ket)sen (i.e., "with the stick chase"). Gillmeister has suggested that not only the name but also the sport itself may be of Flemish origin.

- **Growth of amateur and professional cricket in England**

Evolution of the cricket bat. The original "hockey stick" (left) evolved into the straight bat from c. 1760 when pitched delivery bowling began.

Although the main object of the game has always been to score the most runs, the early form of cricket differed from the modern game in certain key technical aspects; the North American variant of cricket known as wicket retained many of these aspects. The ball was bowled underarm by the bowler and along the ground towards a batter armed with a bat that in shape resembled a hockey stick; the batter defended a low, two-stump wicket; and runs were called notches because the scorers recorded them by notching tally sticks.

In 1611, the year Cotgrave's dictionary was published, ecclesiastical court records at Sidlesham in Sussex state that two parishioners, Bartholomew Wyatt and Richard Latter, failed to attend church on Easter Sunday because they were playing cricket. They were fined 12d each and ordered to do penance.This is the earliest mention of adult participation in cricket and it was around the same time that the earliest known organised inter-parish or village match was played – at Chevening, Kent. In 1624, a player called Jasper Vinall died after he was accidentally struck on the head during a match between two parish teams in Sussex.

Cricket remained a low-key local pursuit for much of the 17th century. It is known, through numerous references found in the records of ecclesiastical court cases, to have been proscribed at times by the Puritans before and during the Commonwealth. The problem was nearly always the issue of Sunday play as the Puritans considered cricket to be "profane" if played on the Sabbath, especially if large crowds or gambling were involved.

According to the social historian Derek Birley, there was a "great upsurge of sport after the Restoration" in 1660. Gambling on sport became a problem significant enough for Parliament to pass the 1664 Gambling Act, limiting stakes to £100 which was, in any case, a colossal sum exceeding the annual income of 99% of the population. Along with prizefighting, horse racing and blood sports, cricket was perceived to be a gambling sport.Rich patrons made matches for high stakes, forming teams in which they engaged the first professional players.By the end of the century, cricket had developed into a major sport that was spreading throughout England and was already being taken abroad by English mariners and colonisers – the earliest reference to cricket overseas is dated 1676. A 1697 newspaper report survives of "a great cricket match" played in Sussex "for fifty guineas apiece" – this is the earliest known contest that is generally considered a First Class match.

- The patrons, and other players from the social class known as the "gentry", began to classify themselves as "amateurs" to establish a clear distinction from the professionals, who were invariably members of the working class, even to the point of having separate changing and dining facilities. The gentry, including such high-ranking nobles as the Dukes of Richmond, exerted their honour code of noblesse oblige to claim rights of leadership in any sporting contests they took part in, especially as it was necessary for them to play alongside their "social inferiors" if they were to win their bets. In time, a perception took hold that the typical amateur who played in first-class cricket, until 1962 when amateurism was abolished, was someone with a public school education who had then gone to one of Cambridge or Oxford University – society insisted that such people were "officers and gentlemen" whose destiny was to provide leadership. In a purely financial sense, the cricketing amateur would theoretically claim expenses for playing while his professional counterpart played under contract and was paid a wage or match fee;

in practice, many amateurs claimed more than actual expenditure and the derisive term "shamateur" was coined to describe the practice.

· The Young Cricketer, 1768

The game underwent major development in the 18th century to become England's national sport.Its success was underwritten by the twin necessities of patronage and betting. Cricket was prominent in London as early as 1707 and, in the middle years of the century, large crowds flocked to matches on the Artillery Ground in Finsbury. The single wicket form of the sport attracted huge crowds and wagers to match, its popularity peaking in the 1748 season. Bowling underwent an evolution around 1760 when bowlers began to pitch the ball instead of rolling or skimming it towards the batter. This caused a revolution in bat design because, to deal with the bouncing ball, it was necessary to introduce the modern straight bat in place of the old "hockey stick" shape.

The Hambledon Club was founded in the 1760s and, for the next twenty years until the formation of Marylebone Cricket Club (MCC) and the opening of Lord's Old Ground in 1787, Hambledon was both the game's greatest club and its focal point. MCC quickly became the sport's premier club and the custodian of the Laws of Cricket. New Laws introduced in the latter part of the 18th century included the three stump wicket and leg before wicket (lbw).

The 19th century saw underarm bowling superseded by first roundarm and then overarm bowling. Both developments were controversial.Organisation of the game at county level led to the creation of the county clubs, starting with Sussex in 1839. In December 1889, the eight leading county clubs formed the official County Championship, which began in 1890.

The most famous player of the 19th century was W. G. Grace, who started his long and influential career in 1865. It was especially during the career of Grace that the distinction between amateurs and professionals became blurred by the existence of players like him who were nominally amateur but, in terms of their financial gain, de facto professional. Grace himself was said to have been paid more money for playing cricket than any professional.

The last two decades before the First World War have been called the "Golden Age of cricket". It is a nostalgic name prompted by the collective sense of loss resulting from the war, but the period did produce some great players and memorable matches, especially as organised competition at county and Test level developed.

· Cricket becomes an international sport

In 1844, the first-ever international match took place between the United States and Canada. In 1859, a team of English players went to North America on the first overseas tour. Meanwhile, the British Empire had been instrumental in spreading the game overseas and by the middle of the 19th century it had become well established in Australia, the Caribbean, India, Pakistan, New Zealand, North America and South Africa.

In 1862, an English team made the first tour of Australia. The first Australian team to travel overseas consisted of Aboriginal stockmen who toured England in 1868. The first One Day International match was played on 5 January 1971 between Australia and England at the Melbourne Cricket Ground.

In 1876–77, an England team took part in what was retrospectively recognised as the first-ever Test match at the Melbourne Cricket Ground against Australia. The rivalry between England and Australia gave birth to The Ashes in 1882, and this has remained Test cricket's most famous contest. Test cricket began to expand in 1888–89 when South Africa played England.

· World cricket in the 20th century

The inter-war years were dominated by Australia's Don Bradman, statistically the greatest Test batter of all time. Test cricket continued to expand during the 20th century with the addition of the West Indies (1928), New Zealand (1930) and India (1932) before the Second World War and then Pakistan (1952), Sri Lanka (1982), Zimbabwe (1992), Bangladesh (2000), Ireland and Afghanistan (both 2018) in the post-war period. South Africa was banned from international cricket from 1970 to 1992 as part of the apartheid boycott.

· The rise of limited overs cricket

Cricket entered a new era in 1963 when English counties introduced the limited overs variant. As it was sure to produce a result, limited overs cricket was lucrative and the number of matches increased. The first Limited Overs International was played in 1971 and the governing International Cricket Council (ICC), seeing its potential, staged the first limited overs Cricket World Cup in 1975. In the 21st century, a new limited overs form, Twenty20, made an immediate impact. On 22 June 2017, Afghanistan and Ireland became the 11th and 12th ICC full members, enabling them to play Test cricket.

· A typical cricket field.

In cricket, the rules of the game are specified in a code called The Laws of Cricket (hereinafter called "the Laws") which has a global remit. There are 42 Laws (always written with a capital "L"). The earliest known version of the code was drafted in 1744 and, since 1788, it has been owned and maintained by its custodian, the Marylebone Cricket Club (MCC) in London.

· Playing area

Cricket is a bat-and-ball game played on a cricket field between two teams of eleven players each. The field is usually circular or oval in shape and the edge of the playing area is marked by a boundary, which may be a fence, part of the stands, a rope, a painted line or a combination of these; the boundary must if possible be marked along its entire length.

In the approximate centre of the field is a rectangular pitch (see image, below) on which a wooden target called a wicket is sited at each end; the wickets are placed 22 yards (20 m) apart. The pitch is a flat surface 10 feet (3.0 m) wide, with very short grass that tends to be worn away as the game progresses (cricket can also be played on artificial surfaces, notably matting). Each wicket is made of three wooden stumps topped by two bails.

· Cricket pitch and creases

As illustrated above, the pitch is marked at each end with four white painted lines: a bowling crease, a popping crease and two return creases. The three stumps are aligned centrally on the bowling crease, which is eight feet eight inches long. The popping crease is drawn four feet in front of the bowling crease and parallel to it; although it is drawn as a twelve-foot line (six feet either side of the wicket), it is, in fact, unlimited in length. The return creases are drawn at right angles to the popping crease so that they intersect the ends of the bowling crease; each return crease is drawn as an eight-foot line, so that it extends four feet behind the bowling crease, but is also, in fact, unlimited in length.

Before a match begins, the team captains (who are also players) toss a coin to decide which team will bat first and so take the first innings. Innings is the term used for each phase of play in the match.In each innings, one team bats, attempting to score runs, while the other team bowls and fields the ball, attempting to restrict the scoring and dismiss the batters. When the first innings ends, the teams change roles; there can be two to four innings depending upon the type of match. A match with four scheduled innings is played over three to five days; a match with two scheduled innings is usually completed in a single day. During an innings, all eleven members of the fielding team take the field, but usually only two members of the batting team are on the field at any given time. The exception to this is if a batter has any type of illness or injury restricting his or her ability to run, in this case the batter is allowed a runner who can run between the wickets when the batter hits a scoring run or runs,though this does not apply in international cricket. The order of batters is usually announced just before the match, but it can be varied.

The main objective of each team is to score more runs than their opponents but, in some forms of cricket, it is also necessary to dismiss all of the opposition batters in their final innings in order to win the match, which would otherwise be drawn. If the team batting last is all out having scored fewer runs than their opponents, they are said to have "lost by n runs" (where n is the difference between the aggregate number of runs scored by the teams). If the team that bats last scores enough runs to win, it is said to have "won by n wickets", where n is the number of wickets left to fall. For example, a team that passes its opponents' total having lost six wickets (i.e., six of their batters have been dismissed) have won the match "by four wickets".

In a two-innings-a-side match, one team's combined first and second innings total may be less than the other side's first innings total. The team with the greater score is then said to have "won by an innings and n runs", and does not need to bat again: n is the difference between the two teams' aggregate scores. If the team batting last is all out, and both sides have scored the same number of runs, then the match is a tie; this result is quite rare in matches of two innings a side with only 62 happening in first-class matches from the earliest known instance in 1741 until January 2017. In the traditional form of the game, if the time allotted for the match expires before either side can win, then the game is declared a draw.

If the match has only a single innings per side, then a maximum number of overs applies to each innings. Such a match is called a "limited overs" or "one-day" match, and the side scoring more runs wins regardless of the number of wickets lost, so that a draw cannot occur. In some cases, ties are broken by having each team bat for a one-over innings known as a Super Over; subsequent Super Overs may be played if the first Super Over ends in a tie. If this kind of match is temporarily interrupted by bad weather, then a complex mathematical formula, known as the Duckworth–Lewis–Stern method after its developers, is often used to recalculate a new target score. A one-day match can also be declared a "no-result" if fewer than a previously agreed number of overs have been bowled by either team, in circumstances that make normal resumption of play impossible; for example, wet weather.

In all forms of cricket, the umpires can abandon the match if bad light or rain makes it impossible to continue. There have been instances of entire matches, even Test matches scheduled to be played over five days, being lost to bad weather without a ball being bowled: for example, the third Test of the 1970/71 series in Australia.

· **Innings**

The innings (ending with 's' in both singular and plural form) is the term used for each phase of play during a match. Depending on the type of match being played, each team has either one or two innings. Sometimes all eleven members of the batting side take a turn to bat but, for various reasons, an innings can end before they have all done so. The innings terminates if the batting team is "all out", a term defined by the Laws: "at the fall of a wicket or the retirement of a batter, further balls remain to be bowled but no further batter is available to come in". In this situation, one of the batters has not been dismissed and is termed not out; this is because he has no partners left and there must always be two active batters while the innings is in progress.

- **An innings may end early while there are still two not out batters**

the batting team's captain may declare the innings closed even though some of his players have not had a turn to bat: this is a tactical decision by the captain, usually because he believes his team have scored sufficient runs and need time to dismiss the opposition in their innings

the set number of overs (i.e., in a limited overs match) have been bowled

the match has ended prematurely due to bad weather or running out of time

in the final innings of the match, the batting side has reached its target and won the game.

- **Overs**

The Laws state that, throughout an innings, "the ball shall be bowled from each end alternately in overs of 6 balls". The name "over" came about because the umpire calls "Over!" when six balls have been bowled. At this point, another bowler is deployed at the other end, and the fielding side changes ends while the batters do not. A bowler cannot bowl two successive overs, although a bowler can (and usually does) bowl alternate overs, from the same end, for several overs which are termed a "spell". The batters do not change ends at the end of the over, and so the one who was non-striker is now the striker and vice versa. The umpires also change positions so that the one who was at "square leg" now stands behind the wicket at the non-striker's end and vice versa.

- **Clothing and equipment**

English cricketer W. G. Grace "taking guard" in 1883. His pads and bat are very similar to those used today. The gloves have evolved somewhat. Many modern players use more defensive equipment than were available to Grace, most notably helmets and arm guards.

The wicket-keeper (a specialised fielder behind the batter) and the batters wear protective gear because of the hardness of the ball, which can be delivered at speeds of more than 145 kilometres per hour (90 mph) and presents a major health and safety concern. Protective clothing includes pads (designed to protect the knees and shins), batting gloves or wicket-keeper's gloves for the hands, a safety helmet for the head and a box for male players inside the trousers (to protect the crotch area). Some batters wear additional padding inside their shirts and trousers such as thigh pads, arm pads, rib protectors and shoulder pads. The only fielders allowed to wear protective gear are those in positions very close to the batter (i.e., if they are alongside or in front of him), but they cannot wear gloves or external leg guards.

Subject to certain variations, on-field clothing generally includes a collared shirt with short or long sleeves; long trousers; woolen pullover (if needed); cricket cap (for fielding) or a safety helmet; and spiked shoes or boots to increase traction. The kit is traditionally all white and this remains the case in Test and first-class cricket but, in limited overs cricket, team colours are worn instead.

· **Bat and ball**

Two types of cricket ball, both of the same size:
i) A used white ball. White balls are mainly used in limited overs cricket, especially in matches played at night,

under floodlights (left).

ii) A used red ball. Red balls are used in Test cricket, first-class cricket and some other forms of cricket (right).

The essence of the sport is that a bowler delivers (i.e., bowls) the ball from his or her end of the pitch towards the batter who, armed with a bat, is "on strike" at the other end (see next sub-section: Basic gameplay).

The bat is made of wood, usually Salix alba (white willow), and has the shape of a blade topped by a cylindrical handle. The blade must not be more than 4.25 inches (10.8 cm) wide and the total length of the bat not more than 38 inches (97 cm). There is no standard for the weight, which is usually between 2 lb 7 oz and 3 lb (1.1 and 1.4 kg).

The ball is a hard leather-seamed spheroid, with a circumference of 9 inches (23 cm). The ball has a "seam": six rows of stitches attaching the leather shell of the ball to the string and cork interior. The seam on a new ball is prominent and helps the bowler propel it in a less predictable manner. During matches, the quality of the ball deteriorates to a point where it is no longer usable; during the course of this deterioration, its behaviour in flight will change and can influence the outcome of the match. Players will, therefore, attempt to modify the ball's behaviour by modifying its physical properties. Polishing the ball and wetting it with sweat or saliva is legal, even when the polishing is deliberately done on one side only to increase the ball's swing through the air, but the acts of rubbing other substances into the ball, scratching the surface or picking at the seam are illegal ball tampering.

· **Player roles**

Basic gameplay: bowler to batter

During normal play, thirteen players and two umpires are on the field. Two of the players are batters and the rest are all eleven members of the fielding team. The other nine players in the batting team are off the field in the pavilion. The image with overlay below shows what is happening when a ball is being bowled and which of the personnel are on or close to the pitch.

- **Return crease**

In the photo, the two batters (3 & 8; wearing yellow) have taken position at each end of the pitch (6). Three members of the fielding team (4, 10 & 11; wearing dark blue) are in shot. One of the two umpires (1; wearing white hat) is stationed behind the wicket (2) at the bowler's (4) end of the pitch. The bowler (4) is bowling the ball (5) from his end of the pitch to the batter at the other end who is called the "striker". The other batter (3) at the bowling end is called the "non-striker". The wicket-keeper (10), who is a specialist, is positioned behind the striker's wicket (9) and behind him stands one of the fielders in a position called "first slip" (11). While the bowler and the first slip are wearing conventional kit only, the two batters and the wicket-keeper are wearing protective gear including safety helmets, padded gloves and leg guards (pads).

While the umpire (1) in shot stands at the bowler's end of the pitch, his colleague stands in the outfield, usually in or near the fielding position called "square leg", so that he is in line with the popping crease (7) at the striker's end of the pitch. The bowling crease (not numbered) is the one on which the wicket is located between the return creases (12). The bowler (4) intends to hit the wicket (9) with the ball (5) or, at least, to prevent the striker (8) from scoring runs. The striker (8) intends, by using his bat, to defend his wicket and, if possible, to hit the ball away from the pitch in order to score runs.

Some players are skilled in both batting and bowling, or as either or these as well as wicket-keeping, so are termed all-rounders. Bowlers are classified according to their style, generally as fast bowlers, seam bowlers or spinners. Batters are classified according to whether they are right-handed or left-handed.

· Fielding

Of the eleven fielders, three are in shot in the image above. The other eight are elsewhere on the field, their positions determined on a tactical basis by the captain or the bowler. Fielders often change position between deliveries, again as directed by the captain or bowler.

If a fielder is injured or becomes ill during a match, a substitute is allowed to field instead of him, but the substitute cannot bowl or act as a captain, except in the case of concussion substitutes in international cricket. The substitute leaves the field when the injured player is fit to return. The Laws of Cricket were updated in 2017 to allow substitutes to act as wicket-keepers.

· Bowling and dismissal

Glenn McGrath of Australia holds the world record for most wickets in the Cricket World Cup.

Most bowlers are considered specialists in that they are selected for the team because of their skill as a bowler, although some are all-rounders and even specialist batters bowl occasionally. The specialists bowl several times during an innings but may not bowl two overs consecutively. If the captain wants a bowler to "change ends", another bowler must temporarily fill in so that the change is not immediate.

A bowler reaches his delivery stride by means of a "run-up" and an over is deemed to have begun when the bowler starts his run-up for the first delivery of that over, the ball then being "in play".

Fast bowlers, needing momentum, take a lengthy run up while bowlers with a slow delivery take no more than a couple of steps before bowling. The fastest bowlers can deliver the ball at a speed of over 145 kilometres per hour (90 mph) and they sometimes rely on sheer speed to try to defeat the batter, who is forced to react very quickly.

Other fast bowlers rely on a mixture of speed and guile by making the ball seam or swing (i.e. curve) in flight. This type of delivery can deceive a batter into miscuing his shot, for example, so that the ball just touches the edge of the bat and can then be "caught behind" by the wicket-keeper or a slip fielder. At the other end of the bowling scale is the spin bowler who bowls at a relatively slow pace and relies entirely on guile to deceive the batter. A spinner will often "buy his wicket" by "tossing one up" (in a slower, steeper parabolic path) to lure the batter into making a poor shot. The batter has to be very wary of such deliveries as they are often "flighted" or spun so that the ball will not behave quite as he expects and he could be "trapped" into getting himself out. In between the pacemen and the spinners are the medium paced seamers who rely on persistent accuracy to try to contain the rate of scoring and wear down the batter's concentration.

There are nine ways in which a batter can be dismissed: five relatively common and four extremely rare. The common forms of dismissal are bowled, caught, leg before wicket (lbw), run out and stumped. Rare methods are hit wicket,hit the ball twice, obstructing the field and timed out. The Laws state that the fielding team, usually the bowler in practice, must appeal for a dismissal before the umpire can give his decision. If the batter is out, the umpire raises a forefinger and says "Out!"; otherwise, he will shake his head and say "Not out".There is, effectively, a tenth method of dismissal, retired out, which is not an on-field dismissal as such but rather a retrospective one for which no fielder is credited.

- **Batting, runs and extras**

The directions in which a right-handed batter, facing down the page, intends to send the ball when playing various cricketing shots. The diagram for a left-handed batter is a mirror image of this one.

Batters take turns to bat via a batting order which is decided beforehand by the team captain and presented to the umpires, though the order remains flexible when the captain officially nominates the team. Substitute batters are generally not allowed, except in the case of concussion substitutes in international cricket.

In order to begin batting the batter first adopts a batting stance. Standardly, this involves adopting a slight crouch with the feet pointing across the front of the wicket, looking in the direction of the bowler, and holding the bat so it passes over the feet and so its tip can rest on the ground near to the toes of the back foot.

A skilled batter can use a wide array of "shots" or "strokes" in both defensive and attacking mode. The idea is to hit the ball to the best effect with the flat surface of the bat's blade. If the ball touches the side of the bat it is called an "edge". The batter does not have to play a shot and can allow the ball to go through to the wicketkeeper. Equally, he does not have to attempt a run when he hits the ball with his bat. Batters do not always seek to hit the ball as hard as possible, and a good player can score runs just by making a deft stroke with a turn of the wrists or by simply "blocking" the ball but directing it away from fielders so that he has time to take a run. A wide variety of shots are played, the batter's repertoire including strokes named according to the style of swing and the direction aimed: e.g., "cut", "drive", "hook", "pull".

The batter on strike (i.e. the "striker") must prevent the ball hitting the wicket, and try to score runs by hitting the ball with his bat so that he and his partner have time to run from one end of the pitch to the other before the fielding side can return the ball. To register a run, both runners must touch the ground behind the popping crease with either their bats or their bodies (the batters carry their bats as they run). Each completed run increments the score of both the team and the striker.

- **Sachin Tendulkar is the only player to have scored one hundred international centuries**

The decision to attempt a run is ideally made by the batter who has the better view of the ball's progress, and this is communicated by calling: usually "yes", "no" or "wait". More than one run can be scored from a single hit: hits worth one to three runs are common, but the size of the field is such that it is usually difficult to run four or more. To compensate for this, hits that reach the boundary of the field are automatically awarded four runs if the ball touches the ground en route to the boundary or six runs if the ball clears the boundary without touching the ground within the boundary. In these cases the batters do not need to run. Hits for five are unusual and generally rely on the help of "overthrows" by a fielder returning the ball. If an odd number of runs is scored by the striker, the two batters have changed ends, and the one who was non-striker is now the striker. Only the striker can score individual runs, but all runs are added to the team's total.

Additional runs can be gained by the batting team as extras (called "sundries" in Australia) due to errors made by the fielding side. This is achieved in four ways: no-ball, a penalty of one extra conceded by the bowler if he breaks the rules; wide, a penalty of one extra conceded by the bowler if he bowls so that the ball is out of the batter's reach bye, an extra awarded if the batter misses the ball and it goes past the wicket-keeper and gives the batters time to run in the conventional way leg bye, as for a bye except that the ball has hit the batter's body, though not his bat. If the bowler has conceded a no-ball or a wide, his team incurs an additional penalty because that ball (i.e., delivery) has to be bowled again and hence the batting side has the opportunity to score more runs from this extra ball.

- **Specialist roles**

Captain (cricket) and Wicket-keeper

The captain is often the most experienced player in the team, certainly the most tactically astute, and can possess any of the main skillsets as a batter, a bowler or a wicket-keeper. Within the Laws, the captain has certain responsibilities in terms of nominating his players to the umpires before the match and ensuring that his players conduct themselves "within the spirit and traditions of the game as well as within the Laws".

The wicket-keeper (sometimes called simply the "keeper") is a specialist fielder subject to various rules within the Laws about his equipment and demeanour. He is the only member of the fielding side who can effect a stumping and is the only one permitted to wear gloves and external leg guards. Depending on their primary skills, the other ten players in the team tend to be classified as specialist batters or specialist bowlers. Generally, a team will include five or six specialist batters and four or five specialist bowlers, plus the wicket-keeper.

· Umpires and scorers

The game on the field is regulated by the two umpires, one of whom stands behind the wicket at the bowler's end, the other in a position called "square leg" which is about 15–20 metres away from the batter on strike and in line with the popping crease on which he is taking guard. The umpires have several responsibilities including adjudication on whether a ball has been correctly bowled (i.e., not a no-ball or a wide); when a run is scored; whether a batter is out (the fielding side must first appeal to the umpire, usually with the phrase "How's that?" or "Owzat?"); when intervals start and end; and the suitability of the pitch, field and weather for playing the game. The umpires are authorised to interrupt or even abandon a match due to circumstances likely to endanger the players, such as a damp pitch or deterioration of the light.

Off the field in televised matches, there is usually a third umpire who can make decisions on certain incidents with the aid of video evidence. The third umpire is mandatory under the playing conditions for Test and Limited Overs

International matches played between two ICC full member countries. These matches also have a match referee whose job is to ensure that play is within the Laws and the spirit of the game.

The match details, including runs and dismissals, are recorded by two official scorers, one representing each team. The scorers are directed by the hand signals of an umpire . For example, the umpire raises a forefinger to signal that the batter is out (has been dismissed); he raises both arms above his head if the batter has hit the ball for six runs. The scorers are required by the Laws to record all runs scored, wickets taken and overs bowled; in practice, they also note significant amounts of additional data relating to the game.

A match's statistics are summarised on a scorecard. Prior to the popularisation of scorecards, most scoring was done by men sitting on vantage points cuttings notches on tally sticks and runs were originally called notches.According to Rowland Bowen, the earliest known scorecard templates were introduced in 1776 by T. Pratt of Sevenoaks and soon came into general use.It is believed that scorecards were printed and sold at Lord's for the first time in 1846.

THREE

ENGLAND CRICKET TEAM

- **England cricket team**

The England cricket team represents England and Wales in international cricket. Since 1997, it has been governed by the England and Wales Cricket Board (ECB), having been previously governed by Marylebone Cricket Club (the MCC) since 1903. England, as a founding nation, is a Full Member of the International Cricket Council (ICC) with Test, One Day International (ODI) and Twenty20 International (T20I) status. Until the 1990s, Scottish and Irish players also played for England as those countries were not yet ICC members in their own right.

England and Australia were the first teams to play a Test match (15–19 March 1877), and along with South Africa, these nations formed the Imperial Cricket Conference (the predecessor to today's International Cricket Council) on 15 June 1909. England and Australia also played the first ODI on 5 January 1971. England's first T20I was played on 13 June

2005, once more against Australia.

As of 20 December 2022, England have played 1,058 Test matches, winning 387 and losing 317 (with 354 draws). In Test series against Australia, England play for The Ashes, one of the most famous trophies in all of sport, and they have won the urn on 32 occasions. England have also played 773 ODIs, winning 389. They have appeared in the final of the Cricket World Cup four times, winning once in 2019; they have also finished as runners-up in two ICC Champions Trophies (2004 and 2013). England have played 170 T20Is, winning 90. They won the ICC T20 World Cup in 2010 and 2022, and were runners-up in 2016.As of 20 December 2022, England are ranked third in Tests, second in ODIs and second in T20Is by the ICC.

- **The All-England Eleven in 1846**

The first recorded incidence of a team with a claim to represent England comes from 9 July 1739 when an "All-England" team, which consisted of 11 gentlemen from any part of England exclusive of Kent, played against "the Unconquerable County" of Kent and lost by a margin of "very few notches". Such matches were repeated on numerous occasions for the best part of a century.In 1846 William Clarke formed the All-England Eleven. This team eventually competed against a United All-England Eleven with annual matches occurring between 1847 and 1856. These matches were arguably the most important contest of the English season if judged by the quality of the players.

- **The 1859 English team to North America.**

The first overseas tour occurred in September 1859 with England touring North America. This team had six players from the All-England Eleven, six from the United All-England Eleven and was captained by George Parr. With the outbreak of the American Civil War, attention turned elsewhere. English tourists visited Australia in 1861–62 with this first tour organised as a commercial venture by Messrs Spiers and Pond, restaurateurs of Melbourne. Most matches played during tours prior to 1877 were "against odds", with the opposing team fielding more than 11 players to make for a more even contest. This first Australian tour were mostly against odds of at least 18/11.

- **The first England team to tour southern Australia in 1861–62**

The tour was so successful that Parr led a second tour in 1863–64. James Lillywhite led a subsequent England team which sailed on the P&O steamship Poonah on 21 September 1876. They played a combined Australian XI, for once on even terms of 11-a-side. The match, starting on 15 March 1877 at the Melbourne Cricket Ground came to be regarded as the inaugural Test match. The combined Australian XI won this Test match by 45 runs with Charles Bannerman of Australia scoring the first Test century. At the time, the match was promoted as James Lillywhite's XI v Combined Victoria and New South Wales. The teams played a return match on the same ground at Easter, 1877, when Lillywhite's team avenged their loss with a victory by four wickets. The first Test match on English soil occurred in 1880 with England victorious; this was the first time England fielded a fully representative side with W. G. Grace included in the team.

- **1880s**

As a result of this loss, the tour of 1882–83 was dubbed by England captain Ivo Bligh as "the quest to regain the ashes". England, with a mixture of amateurs and professionals, won the series 2–1. Bligh was presented with an urn that contained some ashes, which have variously been said to be of a bail, ball or even a woman's veil, and so The Ashes was born. A fourth match was then played which Australia won by four wickets. However, the match was not considered part of the Ashes series. England dominated many of these early contests, with England winning the Ashes series 10 times between 1884 and 1898. During this period England also played their first Test match against South Africa in 1889 at Port Elizabeth.

- **1890s**

England won the 1890 Ashes series 2–0, with the third match of the series being the first Test match to be abandoned. England lost 2–1 in the 1891–92 series, although England regained the urn the following year. England again won the 1894–95 series, winning 3–2 under the leadership of Andrew Stoddart. In 1895–96, England played South Africa, winning all Tests in the series. The 1899 Ashes series was the first tour where the MCC and the counties appointed a selection committee. There were three active players: Grace, Lord Hawke and Warwickshire captain Herbert Bainbridge. Prior to this, England teams for home Tests had been chosen by the club on whose ground the match was to be played. England lost the 1899 Ashes series 1–0, with Grace making his final Test appearance in the first match of the series.

· **1900s**

The start of the 20th century saw mixed results for England as they lost four of the eight Ashes series between 1900 and 1914. During this period, England lost their first series against South Africa in the 1905–06 season 4–1 as their batting faltered.England lost their first series of the new century to Australia in 1901–02 Ashes. Australia also won the 1902 series, which was memorable for exciting cricket, including Gilbert Jessop scoring a Test century in just 70 minutes. England regained the Ashes in 1904 under the captaincy of Pelham Warner. R. E. Foster scored 287 on his debut and Wilfred Rhodes took 15 wickets in a match. In 1905–06, England lost 4–1 against South Africa. England avenged the defeat in 1907, when they won the series 1–0 under the captaincy of Foster. However, they lost the 1909 Ashes series against Australia, suing 25 players in the process. England also lost to South Africa, with Jack Hobbs scoring his first of 15 centuries on the tour.

· **1910s**

England toured Australia in 1911–12 and beat their opponents 4–1. The team included the likes of Rhodes, Hobbs, Frank Woolley and Sydney Barnes. England lost the first match of the series but bounced back and won the next four Tests. This proved to be the last Ashes series before the war.The 1912 season saw England take part in a unique experiment. A nine-Test triangular tournament involving England, South Africa and Australia was set up. The series was hampered by a very wet summer and player disputes however and the tournament was considered a failure with the Daily Telegraph stating.Nine Tests provide a surfeit of cricket, and contests between Australia and South Africa are not a great attraction to the British public.

With Australia sending a weakened team and the South African bowlers being ineffective England dominated the tournament winning four of their six matches. The match between Australia and South Africa at Lord's was visited by King George V, the first time a reigning monarch had watched Test cricket. England went on one more tour before the outbreak of the First World War, beating South Africa 4–0, with Barnes taking 49 wickets in the series.

· **1920s**

English cricket team at the Test match at the Brisbane Exhibition Ground in 1928. England won by a record margin of 675 runs.England's first match after the war was in the 1920–21 season against Australia. Still feeling the effects of the war England went down to a series of crushing defeats and suffered their first whitewash losing the series 5–0. Six Australians scored hundreds while Mailey spun out 36 English batsmen. Things were no better in the next few Ashes series losing the 1921 Ashes series 3–0 and the 1924–25 Ashes 4–1. England's fortunes were to change in 1926 as they regained the Ashes and were a formidable team during this period dispatching Australia 4–1 in the 1928–29 Ashes tour.

On the same year the West Indies became the fourth nation to be granted Test status and played their first game against England. England won each of these three Tests by an innings, and a view was expressed in the press that their elevation had proved a mistake although Learie Constantine did the double on the tour. In the 1929–30 season England went on two concurrent tours with one team going to New Zealand (who were granted Test status earlier that year) and the other to the West Indies. Despite sending two separate teams England won both tours beating New Zealand 1–0 and the West Indies 2–1.

· 1930s

Bill Woodfull evades a Bodyline ball. Note the number of leg-side fielders.The 1930 Ashes series saw a young Don Bradman dominate the tour, scoring 974 runs in his seven Test innings. He scored 254 at Lord's, 334 at Headingley and 232 at The Oval. Australia regained the Ashes winning the series 3–1. As a result of Bradman's prolific run-scoring the England captain Douglas Jardine chose to develop the already existing leg theory into fast leg theory, or bodyline, as a tactic to stop Bradman. Fast leg theory involved bowling fast balls directly at the batsman's body. The batsman would need to defend himself, and if he touched the ball with the bat, he risked being caught by one of a large number of fielders placed on the leg side.

Using Jardine's fast leg theory, England won the next Ashes series 4–1, but complaints about the Bodyline tactic caused crowd disruption on the tour, and threats of diplomatic action from the Australian Cricket Board, which during the tour sent the following cable to the MCC in London:

Bodyline bowling assumed such proportions as to menace best interests of game, making protection of body by batsmen the main consideration. Causing intensely bitter feeling between players as well as injury. In our opinion is unsportsmanlike. Unless stopped at once likely to upset friendly relations existing between Australia and England.Later, Jardine was removed from the captaincy and the Laws of Cricket changed so that no more than one fast ball aimed at the body was permitted per over, and having more than two fielders behind square leg was banned.

England's following tour of India in the 1933–34 season was the first Test match to be staged in the subcontinent. The series was also notable for Stan Nichols and Nobby Clark bowling so many bouncers that the Indian batsman wore solar toupées instead of caps to protect themselves.Australia won the 1934 Ashes series 2–1 and kept the urn for the following 19 years. Many of the wickets of the time were friendly to batsmen resulting in a large proportion of matches ending in high scoring draws and many batting records being set.

England drew the 1938 Ashes, meaning Australia retained the urn. England went into the final match of the series at The Oval 1–0 down, but won the final game by an innings and 579 runs. Len Hutton made the highest ever Test score by an Englishman, making 364 in England first innings to help them reach 903, their highest ever score against Australia.

The 1938–39 tour of South Africa saw another experiment with the deciding Test being a timeless Test that was played to a finish. England lead 1–0 going into the final timeless match at Durban. Despite the final Test being 'timeless', the game ended in a draw after 10 days as England had to catch the train to catch the boat home. A record 1,981 runs were scored, and the concept of timeless Tests was abandoned. England went on one final tour of the West Indies in 1939 before the Second World War, although a team for an MCC tour of India was selected more in hope than expectation of the matches being played.

· **1940s**

Test cricket resumed after the war in 1946, and England won their first match back against India. However, they struggled in the 1946–47 Ashes series, losing 3–0 in Australia under Wally Hammond's captaincy. England beat South Africa 3–0 in 1947 with Denis Compton scoring 1,187 runs in the series.

The 1947–48 series against the West Indies was another disappointment for England, with the side losing 2–0 following injuries to several key players. England suffered further humiliation against Bradman's invincible side in the 1948 Ashes series. Hutton was controversially dropped for the third Test, and England were bowled out for just 52 at The Oval. The series proved to be Bradman's final Ashes series.

In 1948–49, England beat South Africa 2–0 under the captaincy of George Mann. The series included a record breaking stand of 359 between Hutton and Cyril Washbrook. The decade ended with England drawing the Test series against New Zealand, with every match ending in a draw.

· **1950s**

Their fortunes changed on the 1953 Ashes tour as they won the series 1–0. England did not lose a series between their 1950–51 and 1958–59 tours of Australia and secured famous victory in 1954–55 under the captaincy of Len Hutton, thanks to Frank Tyson whose 6/85 at Sydney and 7/27 at Melbourne are remembered as the fastest bowling ever seen in Australia. The 1956 series was remembered for the bowling of Jim Laker who took 46 wickets at an average of 9.62, including figures of 19/90 at Old Trafford. After drawing to South Africa, England defeated the West Indies and New Zealand comfortably.

The England team then left for Australia in the 1958–59 season with a team that had been hailed as the strongest ever to leave on an Ashes tour but lost the series 4–0 as Richie Benaud's revitalised Australians were too strong, with England struggling with the bat throughout the series.On 24 August 1959, England inflicted its only 5–0 whitewash over India. All out for 194 at The Oval, India lost the last test by an innings. England's batsman Ken Barrington and Colin Cowdrey both had an excellent series with the bat, with Barrington scoring 357 runs across the series and Cowdrey scoring 344.

· **1960s**

The early and middle 1960s were poor periods for English cricket. Despite England's strength on paper, Australia held the Ashes and the West Indies dominated England in the early part of the decade. May stood down as captain in 1961 following the 1961 Ashes defeat.

Ted Dexter succeeded him as captain but England continued to suffer indifferent results. In 1961–62, they beat Pakistan, but also lost to India. The following year saw England and Australia tie the 1962–63 Ashes series 1–1, meaning Australia retained the urn. Despite beating New Zealand 3–0, England went on to lose to the West Indies, and again failed in the 1964 Ashes, losing the home series 1–0, which marked the end of Dexter's captaincy.

However, from 1968 to 1971 they played 27 consecutive Test matches without defeat, winning 9 and drawing 18 (including the abandoned Test at Melbourne in 1970–71). The sequence began when they drew with Australia at Lord's in the Second Test of the 1968 Ashes series and ended in 1971 when India won the Third Test at The Oval by four wickets. They played 13 Tests with only one defeat immediately beforehand and so played a total of 40 consecutive Tests with only one defeat, dating from their innings victory over the West Indies at The Oval in 1966. During this period they beat New Zealand, India, the West Indies, and Pakistan, and under Ray Illingworth's leadership, regained The Ashes from Australia in 1970–71.

· 1970s

The 1970s, for the England team, can be largely split into three parts. Early in the decade, Illingworth's side dominated world cricket, winning the Ashes away in 1971 and then retaining them at home in 1972. The same side beat Pakistan at home in 1971 and played by far the better cricket against India that season. However, England were largely helped by the rain to sneak the Pakistan series 1–0 but the same rain saved India twice and one England collapse saw them lose to India. This was, however, one of (if not the) strongest England team ever with the likes of Illingworth, Geoffrey Boycott, John Edrich, Basil D'Oliveira, Dennis Amiss, Alan Knott, John Snow and Derek Underwood at its core.

The mid-1970s were more turbulent. Illingworth and several others had refused to tour India in 1972–73 which led to a clamour for Illingworth's job by the end of that summer – England had just been beaten 2–0 by a flamboyant West Indies side – with several England players well over 35. Mike Denness was the surprising choice but only lasted 18 months; his results against poor opposition were good, but England were badly exposed as ageing and lacking in good fast bowling against the 1974–75

Australians, losing that series 4–1 to lose the Ashes.Denness was replaced in 1975 by Tony Greig. While he managed to avoid losing to Australia, his side were largely thrashed the following year by the young and very much upcoming West Indies for whom Greig's infamous "grovel" remark acted as motivation. Greig's finest hour was probably the 1976–77 win over India in India. When Greig was discovered as being instrumental in World Series Cricket, he was sacked, and replaced by Mike Brearley.

Brearley's side showed again the hyperbole that is often spoken when one side dominates in cricket. While his side of 1977–80 contained some young players who went on to become England greats, most notably future captains Ian Botham, David Gower and Graham Gooch, their opponents were often very much weakened by the absence of their World Series players, especially in 1978, when England beat New Zealand 3–0 and Pakistan 2–0 before thrashing what was effectively Australia's 2nd XI 5–1 in 1978–79.

- **1980s**

The England team, with Brearley's exit in 1980, was never truly settled throughout the 1980s, which will probably be remembered as a low point for the team. While some of the great players like Botham, Gooch and Gower had fine careers, the team seldom succeeded in beating good opposition throughout the decade and did not score a home Test victory (except against minnows Sri Lanka) between September 1985 and July 1990.

Botham took over the captaincy in 1980 and they put up a good fight against the West Indies, losing a five match Test series 1–0, although England were humbled in the return series. After scoring a pair in the first Test against Australia,

Botham lost the captaincy due to his poor form, and was replaced by Brearley. Botham returned to form and played exceptionally in the remainder of the series, being named man of the match in the third, fourth and fifth Tests. The series became known as Botham's Ashes as England recorded a 3–1 victory.

Keith Fletcher took over as captain in 1981, but England lost his first series in charge against India. Bob Willis took over as captain in 1982 and enjoyed victories over India and Pakistan, but lost the Ashes after Australia clinched the series 2–1. England hosted the World Cup in 1983 and reached the semi-finals, but their Test form remained poor, as they suffered defeats against New Zealand, Pakistan and the West Indies.Gower took over as skipper in 1984 and led the team to a 2–1 victory over India. They went on to win the 1985 Ashes 3–1, although after this came a poor run of form. Defeat to the West Indies dented the team's confidence, and they went on to lose to India 2–0. In 1986, Micky Stewart was appointed the first full-time England coach. England beat New Zealand, but there was little hope of them retaining the Ashes in 1986–87. However, despite being described as a team that 'can't bat, can't bowl and can't field', they went on to win the series 2–1.

After losing consecutive series against Pakistan, England drew a three match Test series against New Zealand 0–0. They reached the final of the 1987 World Cup, but lost by seven runs against Australia. After losing 4–0 to the West Indies, England lost the Ashes to a resurgent Australia led by Allan Border. With the likes of Gooch banned following a rebel tour to South Africa, a new look England side suffered defeat again against the West Indies, although this time by a margin of 2–1.

· **1990s**

If the 1980s were a low point for English Test cricket, then the 1990s were only a slight improvement. The arrival of Gooch as captain in 1990 forced a move toward more professionalism and especially fitness though it took some time for old habits to die. Even in 2011, one or two successful county players have been shown up as physically unfit for international cricket. Creditable performances against India and New Zealand in 1990 were followed by a hard-fought draw against the 1991 West Indies and a strong performance in the 1992 Cricket World Cup in which the England team finished as runners-up for the second consecutive World Cup, but landmark losses against Australia in 1990–91 and especially Pakistan in 1992 showed England up badly in terms of bowling. So bad was England's bowling in 1993 that Rod Marsh described England's pace attack at one point as "pie throwers". Having lost three of the first four Tests played in England in 1993, Gooch resigned to be replaced by Michael Atherton.

More selectorial problems abounded during Atherton's reign as new chairman of selectors and coach Ray Illingworth (then into his 60s) assumed almost sole responsibility for the team off the field. The youth policy which had seen England emerge from the West Indies tour of 1993–94 with some credit (though losing to a seasoned Windies team) was abandoned and players such as Gatting and Gooch were persisted with when well into their 30s and 40s. England continued to do well at home against weaker opponents such as India, New Zealand and a West Indies side beginning to fade but struggled badly against improving sides like Pakistan and South Africa. Atherton had offered his resignation after losing the 1997 Ashes series 3–2 having been 1–0 up after two matches – eventually to resign one series later in early 1998. England, looking for talent, went through a whole raft of new players during this period, such as Ronnie Irani, Adam Hollioake, Craig White, Graeme Hick and Mark Ramprakash. At this time, there were two main problems:

The lack of a genuine all-rounder to bat at 6, Botham having left a huge gap in the batting order when he retired from Tests in 1992.Alec Stewart, a sound wicket-keeper and an excellent player of quick bowling, could not open and keep wicket, hence his batting down the order, where he was often exposed to spin which he did not play as well.

Stewart took the reins as captain in 1998, but another losing Ashes series and early World Cup exit cost him Test and ODI captaincy in 1999. This should not detract from the 1998 home Test series where England showed great fortitude to beat a powerful South African side 2–1.

Another reason for their poor performances were the demands of County Cricket teams on their players, meaning that England could rarely field a full-strength team on their tours. This eventually led to the ECB taking over from the MCC as the governing body of England and the implementation of central contracts. 1992 also saw Scotland sever ties with the England and Wales team, and begin to compete as the Scotland national team.

By 1999, with coach David Lloyd resigning after the World Cup exit and new captain Nasser Hussain just appointed, England hit rock bottom (literally ranked as the lowest-rated Test nation) after losing 2–1 to New Zealand in shambolic fashion. Hussain was booed on the Oval balcony as the crowd jeered "We've got the worst team in the world" to the tune of "He's Got the Whole World in His Hands".

· **2000s**

Central contracts were installed – reducing players workloads – and following the arrival of Zimbabwean coach Duncan Fletcher, England thrashed the fallen West Indies 3–1. England's results in Asia improved that winter with series wins against both Pakistan and Sri Lanka. Hussain's side had a far harder edge to it, avoiding the anticipated "Greenwash" in the 2001 Ashes series against the all-powerful Australian team. The nucleus the side was slowly coming together as players such as Hussain himself, Graham Thorpe, Darren Gough and Ashley Giles began to be regularly selected. By 2003 though, having endured another Ashes drubbing as well as another first-round exit from the World Cup, Hussain resigned as captain after one Test against South Africa.

Michael Vaughan took over, with players encouraged to express themselves. England won five consecutive Test series prior to facing Australia in the 2005 Ashes series, taking the team to second place in the ICC Test Championship table. During this period England defeated the West Indies home and away, New Zealand, and Bangladesh at home, and South Africa in South Africa. In June 2005, England played its first ever T20 international match, defeating Australia by 100 runs. Later that year, England defeated Australia 2–1 in a thrilling series to regain the Ashes for the first time in 16 years, having lost them in 1989. Following the 2005 Ashes win, the team suffered from a spate of serious injuries to key players such as Vaughan, Giles, Andrew Flintoff and Simon Jones. As a result, the team underwent an enforced period of transition. A 2–0 defeat in Pakistan was followed by two drawn away series with India and Sri Lanka.

In the home Test series victory against Pakistan in July and August 2006, several promising new players emerged. Most notable were the left-arm orthodox spin bowler Monty Panesar, the first Sikh to play Test cricket for England, and left-handed opening batsman Alastair Cook. The 2006–07 Ashes series was keenly anticipated and was expected to provide a level of competition comparable to the 2005 series. In the event, England, captained by Flintoff who was deputising for the injured Vaughan, lost all five Tests to concede the first Ashes whitewash in 86 years.

In the 2007 Cricket World Cup, England lost to most of the Test playing nations they faced, beating only the West Indies and Bangladesh, although they also avoided defeat by any of the non-Test playing nations. Even so, the unimpressive nature of most of their victories in the tournament, combined with heavy defeats by New Zealand, Australia and South Africa, left many commentators criticising the manner in which the England team approached the one-day game. Coach Duncan Fletcher resigned after eight years in the job as a result and was succeeded by former Sussex coach Peter Moores.

In 2007–08, England toured Sri Lanka and New Zealand, losing the first series 1–0 and winning the second 2–1. These series were followed up at home in May 2008 with a 2–0 home series win against New Zealand, with the results easing pressure on Moores – who was not at ease with his team, particularly star batsman Kevin Pietersen. Pietersen succeeded Vaughan as captain in June 2008, after England had been well beaten by South Africa at home. The poor relationship between the two came to a head on the 2008–09 tour to India. England lost the series 1–0 and both men resigned their positions, although Pietersen remained a member of the England team. Moores was replaced as coach by Zimbabwean Andy Flower. Against this background, England toured the West Indies under the captaincy of Andrew Strauss and, in a disappointing performance, lost the Test series 1–0.

The 2009 Ashes series featured the first Test match played in Wales, at Sophia Gardens, Cardiff. England drew the match thanks to a last-wicket stand by bowlers James Anderson and Panesar. A victory for each team followed before the series was decided at The Oval. Thanks to fine bowling by Stuart Broad and Graeme Swann and a debut century by Jonathan Trott, England regained the Ashes.

- **2010s**

2019 World cup winning team with prime minister Theresa May After a drawn Test series in South Africa, England won their first ever ICC world championship, the 2010 World Twenty20, with a seven-wicket win over Australia in Barbados. The following winter in the 2010–11 Ashes, they beat Australia 3–1 to retain the urn and record their first series win in Australia for 24 years. Furthermore, all three of their wins were by an innings – the first time a touring side had ever recorded three innings victories in a single Test series. Cook earned Man of the Series with 766 runs.

England struggled to match their Test form in the 2011 Cricket World Cup. Despite beating South Africa and tying with eventual winners India, England suffered shock losses to Ireland and Bangladesh before losing in the quarter-finals to Sri Lanka. However the team's excellent form in the Test match arena continued and on 13 August 2011, they became the world's top-ranked Test team after comfortably whitewashing India 4–0, their sixth consecutive series victory and eighth in the past nine series. However, this status only lasted a year – having lost 3–0 to Pakistan over the winter, England were beaten 2–0 by South Africa, who replaced them at the top of the rankings. It was their first home series loss since 2008, against the same opposition.

This loss saw the resignation of Strauss as captain (and his retirement from cricket). Cook, who was already in charge of the ODI side, replaced Strauss and led England to a 2–1 victory in India – their first in the country since 1984–85. In doing so, he became the first captain to score centuries in his first five Tests as captain and became England's leading century-maker with 23 centuries to his name.

· **The England team celebrate victory over Australia in the 2015 Ashes series**

After finishing as runners-up in the ICC Champions Trophy, England faced Australia in back-to-back Ashes series. A 3–0 home win secured England the urn for the fourth time in five series. However, in the return series, they found themselves utterly demolished in a 5–0 defeat, their second Ashes whitewash in under a decade. Their misery was compounded by batsman Jonathan Trott leaving the tour early due to a stress-related illness and the mid-series retirement of spinner Graeme Swann. Following the tour, head coach Flower resigned his post while Pietersen was dropped indefinitely from the England team. Flower was replaced by his predecessor, Moores, but he was sacked for a second time after a string of disappointing results including failing to advance from the group stage at the 2015 World Cup. He was replaced by Australian Trevor Bayliss who oversaw an upturn of form in the ODI side, including series victories against New Zealand and Pakistan. In the Test arena, England reclaimed the Ashes 3–2 in the summer of 2015.

England entered the 2019 Cricket World Cup as favourites, having been ranked the number one ODI side by the ICC for over a year prior to the tournament. However, shock defeats to Pakistan and Sri Lanka during the group stage left them on the brink of elimination and needing to win their final two games against India and New Zealand to guarantee progression to the semi-finals. This was achieved, putting their campaign back on track, and an eight-wicket victory over Australia in the semi-final at Edgbaston meant England were in their first World Cup final since 1992. The final against New Zealand at Lord's has been described as one of the greatest and most dramatic matches in the history of cricket, with some calling it the "greatest ODI in history", as both the match and subsequent Super Over were tied, after England went into the final over of their innings 14 runs behind New Zealand's total. England won by virtue of having scored more boundaries throughout the match, securing their maiden World Cup title in their fourth final appearance.

· England and Wales Cricket Board

The England and Wales Cricket Board (ECB) is the governing body of English cricket and the England cricket team. The Board has been operating since 1 January 1997 and represents England on the International Cricket Council. The ECB is also responsible for the generation of income from the sale of tickets, sponsorship and broadcasting rights, primarily in relation to the England team. The ECB's income in the 2006 calendar year was £77 million.

Prior to 1997, the Test and County Cricket Board (TCCB) was the governing body for the English team. Apart from in Test matches, when touring abroad, the England team officially played as MCC up to and including the 1976–77 tour of Australia, reflecting the time when MCC had been responsible for selecting the touring party. The last time the England touring team wore the bacon-and-egg colours of the MCC was on the 1996–97 tour of New Zealand.

· **Status of Wales**

Historically, the England team represented the whole of Great Britain in international cricket, with Scottish or Welsh national teams playing sporadically and players from both countries occasionally representing England. Scotland became an independent member of the ICC in 1994, having severed links with the TCCB two years earlier.

Criticism has been made of the England and Wales Cricket Board using only the England name while utilising Welsh players such as Simon and Geraint Jones. With Welsh players pursuing international careers exclusively with an England team, there have been a number of calls for Wales to become an independent member of the ICC, or for the ECB to provide more fixtures for a Welsh national team. However, both Cricket Wales and Glamorgan County Cricket Club have continually supported the ECB, with Glamorgan arguing for the financial benefits of the Welsh county within the English structure, and Cricket Wales stating they are "committed to continuing to play a major role within the ECB"

The absence of a Welsh cricket team has seen a number of debates within the Welsh Senedd. In 2013 a debate saw both Conservative and Labour members lend their support to the establishment of an independent Welsh team.

In 2015, a report produced by the Welsh National Assembly's petitions committee, reflected the passionate debate around the issue. Bethan Jenkins, Plaid Cymru's spokesperson on heritage, culture, sport and broadcasting, and a member of the petitions committee, argued that Wales should have its own international team and withdraw from the ECB. Jenkins noted that Ireland (with a population of 6.4 million) was an ICC member with 6,000 club players whereas Wales (with 3 million) had 7,500. Jenkins said: "Cricket Wales and Glamorgan CCC say the idea of a Welsh national cricket team is 'an emotive subject', of course having a national team is emotive, you only have to look at the stands during any national game to see that. To suggest this as anything other than natural is a bit of a misleading argument."

In 2017, the First Minister of Wales, Carwyn Jones called for the reintroduction of the Welsh one-day team stating: " is odd that we see Ireland and Scotland playing in international tournaments and not Wales."

- **Team colours**

1. 1994–1996Tetley Bitter
2. 1996–1998ASICS
3. 1998–2000Vodafone
4. 2000–2008Admiral
5. 2008–2010Adidas
6. 2010–2014Brit Insurance
7. 2014–2017Waitrose
8. 2017–2021New BalanceNatWest
9. 2021–2022Cinch

10. 2022–presentCastore

In February 2021, England and Wales Cricket Board announced that England's Principal partner NatWest has been replaced by Cinch, an online used car marketplace. England's kit is manufactured by Castore, who replaced previous manufacturer New Balance in April 2022.

When playing Test cricket, England's cricket whites feature the three lions badge on the left of the shirt and the name of the sponsor Cinch on the centre. English fielders may wear a navy blue cap or white sun hat with the ECB logo in the middle. Helmets are also coloured navy blue. Before 1997 the uniform sported the TCCB lion and stumps logo on the uniforms, while the helmets, jumpers and hats had the three lions emblem.

In limited overs cricket, England's ODI and Twenty20 shirts feature the Cinch logo across the centre, with the three lions badge on the left of the shirt and the New Balance logo on the right. In ODIs, the kit comprises a blue shirt with navy trousers, whilst the Twenty20 kit comprises a flame red shirt and navy trousers. In ICC limited-overs tournaments, a modified kit design is used with sponsor's logo moving to the sleeve and 'ENGLAND' printed across the front.Over the years, England's ODI kit has cycled between various shades of blue (such as a pale blue used until the mid-1990s, when it was replaced in favour of a bright blue)with the occasional all-red kit.In April 2017, ECB brought back traditional cable-knit sweater for test matches under new supplier New Balance.

Thank You

Thank You For Reading This Book And Shared This Book To Friends As Birthday Gift Have A Wonderfull Day.